LISTENING BY DOING
Developing Effective Listening Skills

Kathleen Galvin, Ph.D.

NATIONAL TEXTBOOK COMPANY • Lincolnwood, Illinois U.S.A.

Acknowledgments

The Reverend Clements, "Dads, Devote Time to Your Kids," *Chicago Sun-Times,* May 20, 1984. ©News Group Chicago, Inc., 1984. Reprinted with permission of *Chicago Sun-Times.*

Dwight Conquergood, excerpt from "Hmong Pandau—Cloths Made Beautiful Like a Flower." Reprinted by permission of the author.

Ann Diamond, "Between Two Worlds." Reprinted by permission of the author.

Madeline Keen, "I Was in Prison, You Visited Me." Reprinted by permission of the author.

Irving J. Lee and Laura L. Lee. *Handling Barriers in Communication.* New York: Harper & Row, 1968.

Elissa McBride, "Risk It." Reprinted by permission of the author.

National Association for Search and Rescue, "Hug-A-Tree." Published in *National Geographic World,* June 18, 1983.

Judi Silverman, excerpt from "First Person," *Chicago Tribune,* May 6, 1984. Reprinted by permission of the author.

Lisa Sperling, excerpt from "Learn and Live." Reprinted by permission of the author.

Paul Weingarten, excerpt from "First Person," *Chicago Tribune,* January 6, 1984. Reprinted by permission of *Chicago Tribune.*

Preface

Listening is something you do every waking hour of every day. When you are at home, at school, or at work, watching television, talking with friends, or doing almost anything, you are constantly taking in sounds, and you are trying to make sense of them. Listening is the most frequently used communication skill; yet it is the one we take most for granted.

Most people assume that if you have two ears and normal hearing you can listen well. But how often have you heard, "I'm sorry. I didn't get what you said." or "Would you repeat that? I wasn't paying attention." We all make mistakes because we did not listen carefully. Many of these mistakes can be avoided by working to develop good listening skills.

Listening is a basic communication skill that can be improved through knowledge and effort. We see listening as a 5E process involving your *eyes, ears, experience, examination,* and *effort.* In short, we believe good listeners are made, not born.

Each chapter in *Listening by Doing* will help you increase your listening skills. In Chapter 1 you will learn about the process of listening and how it fits within the overall process of communication. In Chapter 2 you will learn to interpret messages more accurately, and you will learn how perceptions affect listening and how to find listening clues in the context of a message. You will also learn about the barriers that keep you from being the best listener possible.

In Chapter 3 you will learn the ways speakers and listeners make things memorable and some strategies for remembering what you just heard. You will learn to become more efficient at following directions. In Chapter 4 you will learn how to find the main points and supporting material in messages. You will also learn ways of organizing spoken messages and how to recognize these organizational patterns while listening to a speaker.

In Chapter 5 you will learn how to listen critically to persuasive messages, how to analyze persuasive appeals, and how to identify propaganda devices. In short, you will learn how to avoid being fooled by a speaker. Finally, in Chapter 6 you will learn how to listen between the words to discover another person's feelings. Then you will learn different ways of responding to feeling messages.

Listening is a skill you will have opportunities to practice in all areas of your life. What you learn in the classroom can be applied to your life as you try to be a good friend, a good worker, a good citizen.

After studying and practicing the skills presented in *Listening by Doing,* you will know that effective listening skills cannot be taken for granted. Good listeners work hard to develop their skills. Don't forget: listening is a skill you will use every day for the rest of your life.

Contents

5 *Analyzing Persuasion*

Listening Practice Section

6 *Listening to Feelings*

"Listening is being silent with another person in an active way."
Morton Kelsey

CHAPTER 1

THE LISTENING PROCESS

Introduction

Most of us take our listening abilities for granted. If we don't have trouble hearing other people, we assume that we listen well. Yet each of us has been involved in situations that became confusing because there was a listening breakdown. Perhaps your English report was late, your friend became angry at you, or you missed the point of a speech. Such confusion tells us that the listening process is not as simple as we may think it is.

Before you begin the study of listening, let's see what you know about the subject already. Read the following statements, and mark each one either T for true or F for false.

1. _____ You can't learn to listen. You are either good at it or not.

2. _____ Listening requires very little effort.

3. _____ The words *listening* and *hearing* mean the same thing.

4. _____ Listening involves only your ears.

5. _____ Listening is an objective process. Your emotions do not affect your ability to listen.

6. _____ You tend to speak more than you listen.

7. _____ Good speakers are usually good listeners.

8. _____ You listen better as you get older.

9. _____ Your need to listen becomes less after you leave school.

10. _____ You listen primarily to get information.

If you marked each of these statements false, you are well on your way to understanding the listening process. Many people believe that ability to listen cannot change; you are either good at it or you are not. But, the real truth is that you can improve your listening ability and enjoy the benefits of your improved listening skill.

Listening by Doing. This may sound like a strange book title, especially since most people believe listening is something that happens *to* you—not something that you *do* actively. In this book, we will view listening as work. In fact, very often listening requires *hard* work. So, when you see the title *Listening by Doing,* it tells you listening is not something that happens within you as when you sit back and relax. It is something you do actively.

In the following pages we will examine: (1) the communication process, (2) the listening process, (3) the purposes for listening, (4) the value of listening.

The Communication Process

Listening is only part of the overall process of communication. Therefore, before we focus on listening specifically, let's look briefly at how the communication process works. Everyone has some idea of what it means to communicate, because we try to do it all the time. We have all been in situations where communication worked well. And we have all experienced breakdowns in communication.

Because communication is a complex process, we could find some very technical definitions. But we don't need those. For our purposes the following definition is useful: *Communication involves the sharing of meanings.*

Sharing

Communication does not work like a beginner's tennis match. In beginning tennis, one person hits the ball over the net and waits for his or her partner to send it back. If communication worked like tennis, the speaker would send a message and then wait for the listener to send one back.

Instead, communication is closer to a skilled tennis match. Both people are involved in the game constantly, just as both tennis players are involved constantly. Once a good player hits the ball, he or she starts to get into position to deal with the return shot. In communication, effective speakers and listeners are always involved. For example, even though a father may appear to talk more than his daughter, she is constantly sending nonverbal signals that affect what he says and does. Both people are involved in every moment of the discussion.

Think about your own conversations. Suppose you and your friend Clare are discussing money. Even as you are speaking to Clare, she is frowning, smiling, looking puzzled, or muttering "uh-huh." She might even interrupt you with a question or a comment. Then, after you finish talking or after you are interrupted, you may be smiling, groaning, or scratching your head while she speaks. Therefore, instead of a stop-start model, we can describe communication as a process of constant involvement. This is important because it shows how the person who is listening is working hard also.

Meanings

Common meanings make it possible for us to communicate. If you and another person do not have the same meanings for words such as "tall," "pretty," "sad," or "soda," you will have difficulty communicating. So too, if you do not have similar meanings for nonverbal messages such as a finger pulled across the neck, a raised eyebrow, a loud tone of voice, there will be confusion.

In this book we will talk about verbal messages (words) and nonverbal messages. Nonverbal messages include the following:
Voice: We may communicate our feelings or moods through the tone of voice we use to talk, or by how fast we talk.
Gestures: We may communicate information or feelings through hand, arm, leg, or head movements.
Body movement: We may communicate information about ourselves or our ideas through posture or movements while walking, standing, or sitting.
Eye Contact and Facial Expression: We may communicate attitudes or feelings through eye contact or facial movements.
Spatial Distances: We may communicate feelings for another person by how much space we put between us and the other person.
Appearance: We may communicate certain feelings or attitudes through style of dress, choice of hair style, and use of accessories such as hats or belts.

As a communicator you use verbal and nonverbal messages to create meanings. For example, you would choose simple words and hand movements to explain star constellations in the sky to your younger brother. You would choose more complex words and gestures to discuss star constellations with your science teacher.

You also need to spend time interpreting the meaning of the messages you receive. You may learn that when Joanna says she'll be "late" that means about fifteen minutes. When Wayne says "late" he means at least an hour. Everyone tries to figure out the right ways to reach another person. Although this appears rather simple and self-evident, it is amazing to see how communication can break down when words or movements or facial expressions are misunderstood.

An effective communicator is aware of nonverbal as well as verbal messages. This person is also aware of how verbal and nonverbal messages work together. We will discuss this in more detail in Chapter 2. Thus, whether you are labeled as a speaker or a listener, you must be aware of your verbal and nonverbal messages.

We said earlier, listening is one part of the communication process. We believe it is an important and underrated part of the process. On the basis of our definition of communication, there are three main ideas to remember about listening:

1. Speaking and listening happen at the same time.

2. Listeners must be aware of both verbal and nonverbal messages.

3. Effective communication occurs when the speakers and listeners share their meanings.

Listening Lab

1. Describe a communication situation in which it is difficult to separate speaking from listening. Use this description as an example.

"I was watching Steve and Carl arguing over baseball at a kitchen table. I quickly realized that speaking and listening are not two totally separate activities. I saw waving arms, heard raised voices and watched them draw pictures in the air with their fingers. Players names and their 1979 batting averages were shouted at each other. At some point I could have called Steve the speaker or sender of the message and called Carl the listener or receiver of the message. But a moment later I could change my mind. They were both talking at once. Carl was carefully listing scores from previous 1979 innings, and Steve was talking about the batting order."

2. Begin a communication journal in which you record: (1) your observations of communication events such as speeches or conversations, (2) your reactions to these events, and (3) questions or concerns about communication.

3. Observe two classmates engaging in a typical cafeteria conversation. Record the activities of the person who is "supposed" to be the listener at particular points. Compare your notes with other observers.
→See Listening Practice 1 on page 99 for further material.

The Listening Process

What do you think about when you think of the word *listening*? Lots of noises coming into your head through your ears? That's a beginning but certainly not the whole story. Listening is more complicated than that.

Listening is a process of *receiving, interpreting, evaluating* and *responding* to messages. It is not just letting sound waves beat on your eardrums. Once you receive a message through your ears, and also through your eyes, you have to work to make sense out of it. You must interpret the message on the basis of your experiences, evaluate your thoughts and/or feelings about the message, and then respond.

All of us listen to machine noises such as a coffeepot perking or a car engine running, and to nature sounds such as waves crashing or birds calling, and to musical sounds such as a soprano singing or a guitarist strumming. Yet, in this book we will be concerned primarily with listening to other people. This includes intentional messages sent by people to other people in a face-to-face situation or through the media. Let's examine how the process really works.

Receiving—Using Your Ears and Eyes

The listening process starts with our senses—primarily our sense of hearing and our sense of sight. We can think of hearing as the physical ability to pick up sound waves through our ears or our biological auditory system. For example, if you are sitting at the kitchen table at 7 A.M., your ears may pick up certain sound waves from the coffeepot dripping, the toaster popping, the TV news, and shoes dropping as sleepy people try to get dressed. In addition, there may be the sounds of talking, laughing or fighting. Yet, you may not be actively aware of each noise. You might be staring at the fascinating cereal box, reading the newspaper, or daydreaming over the orange juice. Only when you shift your attention to concentrate on the television weather news, or to your brother's vocal tone, do you begin to listen. You may even listen very carefully to the TV commentator's description of a record snowfall that may close the schools or to the raised voice of your brother, who suddenly sounds angry. In addition, you may look carefully at the situation more clearly. You will probably look at your brother's face to determine from his expression just how angry he really is at you.

In addition to using our ears to listen, we tend to try to "read" other people's nonverbal signals in order to get the whole message. Our eyes can give us information that helps us interpret the words and vocal tones.

The first step is to use your senses to get the message. For example:

☐ John may tell you, "I'll see you tomorrow at 9."

☐ Mike may state, "Give up your job at Burger Hut for the summer and come work with me at my uncle's resort at the lake. We can earn some money, plus we can sail and swim every day."

☐ Chris may say, "It looks as if my father is going to get remarried."

While each person is talking, you should be tuning out other noise and looking at him or her to pick up any important nonverbal clues.

Interpreting—Tying in Your Experience

Once you have received a message through your ears and eyes, you have to use your own experience to decode what you just heard. As a listener, you must figure out what the message really means. In other words, an effective listener tries to interpret the speaker's message so that the listener truly understands what the speaker has intended. For example:

☐ When John says, "I'll see you at 9 tomorrow," you have to figure out whether he meant 9 A.M. or 9 P.M. You also have to decide if you know where or why he will see you at that time.

☐ When Mike says, "You should give up your job at Burger Hut for the summer and come live with me at my uncle's resort at the lake," you have to think about "my uncle" and "the lake." Which uncle? Which lake?

□ When Chris tells you, "It looks as if my father is going to get remarried," you have to figure out what feeling message goes along with such a big change in Chris's life. Is Chris delighted or unhappy?

While each person is talking, you should be asking yourself, "What does that mean?"

Evaluating—Examining the Message

Once you "get" the message, you have to do something with it. You have to connect that message to your ideas or feelings about that message. You have to decide if you agree or disagree, if you need more information, how you feel about it. For example:

□ You may think, "Oh yeah, band practice at 9 tomorrow, good." Or you may realize that you can't meet John at 9 P.M. because you have a night class then. You may be annoyed that John doesn't remember because you've told him several times that you can't come to band rehearsals if they are held Wednesdays at 9 P.M.

□ You may get very excited about Mike's idea of a summer at the lake. Then, you may start to wonder if you can earn enough money there, and if you can get your Burger Hut job back in September. You may think two months is a long time to be away from your family and other friends.

□ In considering Chris's father's remarriage, you have to think about what she has said about this possibility in the past, if she has mentioned his possible remarriage. You may consider how Chris feels about her father's fiancee as a person.

While each person is talking, you begin to think "so what?" You will ask yourself, "What do I think?" or "How do I feel?" or "What do I need to know?"

Responding—Expending an Effort

A message does not just "plop" in front of you and wait. Almost all messages require a response. The speaker expects a verbal or nonverbal signal that you have heard what he or she has intended to tell you. Now you are faced with sending a verbal/nonverbal response. It can be a simple statement such as "see you then" or a smile. The response may be a question. It may be a long persuasive statement about the subject. It may be a statement that tries to reflect how the other person is feeling, such as, "It's not easy to deal with being a mother and a teacher." A good listener tries to provide some response or feedback. For example:

□ You may respond to John's comment by saying, "See you at 9" or just nodding. You may ask a question, "Didn't we agree to meet on Tuesday this week?" Or you may need to express your feelings, "This is the third time we have met on Wednesday, and you know I have a night class."

□ You might ask Mike about the lake, or the salary, or the sailing. You might say, "I'll do it" or, "I've got to talk to my family and my boss about it." You might say, "I can't go, but thanks for asking."

□ You may find yourself telling Chris, "That's great. I know you like your future stepmom." Or, "Maybe you'll get to like her once you've lived with her." You may reflect your own concern about losing a friend, "Does that mean you will have to move?" On the other hand, your response may be nonverbal—giving her a hug or putting your arm around her shoulder.

The listener's response is critical to effective communication. If the speaker gets no feedback, he or she is separated from you. There is no connection. Recall that true listening involves four steps: *receiving, interpreting, evaluating,* and *responding.*

We can also think of listening as a "5 E" process because it involves:

Ears: We hear words, vocal tones, noises.

Eyes: We see actions, situations, places.

Experience: We relate these messages to our own experience. We interpret the message.

Examination: We make judgments about these messages.

Effort: We respond or give feedback based on our evaluation.

As you go through the steps in the listening process, you should try to use the "5 E's." Your ears and eyes are always working. You rely on your experience to help interpret each message. Each message must be examined in terms of your thoughts and your feelings. Finally, you have to make the effort of responding.

Listening Lab

1. Describe a situation in which you could not interpret the verbal/nonverbal message that you received. For example, someone spoke to you in a language you did not understand, you did not recognize the nonverbal signal, or the noise on the phone line garbled the message. What happened when you could not interpret the message?

2. In your journal describe a situation in which you misinterpreted the words or nonverbal messages you received. What was the real message? How did you misinterpret it? How did you straighten out the confusion?

3. Read the following statements. Assume they are made by a friend of yours. How would you interpret them? How might someone else interpret them differently?

"What are you doing Friday night?"

"Do you have any money with you?"

"Want to go bowling next Monday?"

"Look for a tall guy with a tan jacket and sunglasses."

"It certainly was an interesting play."

4. Read aloud a short quote, (→ *Listening Practice 2, page 99.*) Assume a friend told you this quotation influenced her life. Then do the following:

Ears, Eyes: Receive the message. Could you hear and see the speaker?

Experience: What do you think it means? Can you connect anyone you know to this quotation? How does this tie into your life?

Evaluation: How much sense does this quotation make? Do you think it is wise or idealistic?

Effort: How would you respond to your friend who quoted it to you?

5. Imagine that you are listening to a radio interview show with a guest expert on learning disabilities. The interviewer asks the expert about hyperactivity in children with learning disabilities. The expert gives the following answer: (Someone reads → *Listening Practice 3, page 99.*) How did you listen to the answer? Discuss this in class.

Ears: Could you hear the message?

Experience: What do you think the message means? Could you understand all the words? Could you connect the topic to yourself or to anyone else that you know?

Evaluation: Can you make any judgment about the widsom of the message? Does it seem reasonable? Do you need more information?

Effort: If you were to call the radio show, what would you say?

Purposes of Listening

If someone asked you why you listen, which of these might you answer?

- to be polite

- to get information I need

- to find out how to do something

- to figure out if I want to do something

- to learn things I didn't know before

- to know what I am arguing against

- to show people I care about them

- to make up my mind about controversial subjects

- to enjoy myself

These and other statements are all good reasons for listening to other people. We can examine these reasons more carefully in order to understand why we bother to work at listening. These statements all fall under one of the five major reasons why you may listen:

1. to engage in social rituals

2. to exchange information

3. to exert control

4. to share feelings

5. to enjoy yourself

Engaging in Social Rituals

One practical reason to listen well is to be able to participate in social situations. Each culture or society has its own social rituals or rules for interaction that its members are expected to follow. We have rituals for greetings, for saying goodbye, for small talk for conversations. For example, in a conversation one person should not do all of the talking. You should not stand too close to the other person. You should not talk or listen with your eyes closed. We have rules for communicating in certain settings, such as a classroom or a job interview.

Most Americans expect a listener to maintain eye contact or to look at them most of the time. They also expect a listener to show a physical response, such as nodding, smiling, or frowning, which signals that the listener is thinking about what is being said. In some cultures, good listeners do not look at the speaker's eyes. Instead, the listener looks down as a sign of respect. Or their faces may not show much emotion, because it is not expected.

In every society, a polite listener is expected to act certain ways and to avoid other verbal and nonverbal behavior. Although it may not be the most critical area of listening, the person who is effective in social rituals may develop relationships that lead to more intense and important communication. Think about how hard you work at listening in social situations by answering the following questions.

□ How hard do you try to remember people's names when you are introduced to them or when you hear the names used in conversation?

□ Do you usually make an effort to pay attention when you meet people and you find yourself sharing background information such as interests, place of birth, and so on?

□ How do you feel when you meet a new person and it seems that you have to do all the talking in order to carry the conversation?

Listening Lab

1. Have someone introduce you to three other people using the following model:

"(Your name), this is Joe, whom I told you about. Remember, he's the one who has the snake collection, including a boa that was lost behind the radiator for two weeks. And this is Margaret. Margaret is going to be our concert pianist someday. You should hear her play. And Sam is someone you should know, because you are both interested in stamp collecting. His collection is almost as large as yours, but he probably has stamps from more South American countries than you do. O.K. guys, this is (your name). I've got to run. See you in a while."

Now have someone introduce you to three real people in class using their real names and information about them if you don't know them very well. If you are all well acquainted, have the person make up the names and information. Repeat back the names and information.

2. Pretend that you overhear the following conversation between two people who have just met. Why might they be uncomfortable? What could they do to make the conversation more comfortable?

Pat and Frank are the first to show up at a party given by Ben. Ben has gone to get more food, so Frank and Pat are left alone. Have two people read these:

Pat: Hi, I'm Pat.

Frank: Hi.

Pat: What's your name?

Frank: I'm Frank.

Pat: Are you a friend of Mike's?

Frank: Yes.

Pat: How do you know Mike?

Frank: We play in the same jazz group.

Pat: What do you play?

Frank: I play the sax usually.

Pat: Do you play other instruments, too? I play a little clarinet.

Frank: That's good.

Pat: Where do you study. . .?

Now look at a variation of that conversation and figure out why it worked differently.

Pat: Hi, I'm Pat.

Frank: I'm Frank. Are you a friend of Mike's?

Pat: Yeah. I've known him for about four years. Are you a friend of his also?

Frank: Well, Mike and I know each other through the jazz group. I'm the sax player and he's on the clarinet usually.

Pat: Really? I play clarinet a little myself. I'm not very good yet.

Frank: Hey, you have to start somewhere. Where do you study. . .?

In this example, Pat and Frank are both making an effort to make the conversation comfortable. In our society we expect people to speak, listen, and ask questions when they meet new people. In the first example, Frank let Pat do all of the work. Frank did not seem interested in Pat and did not provide much information. Pat then had to work very hard.

3. The following list contains a number of behaviors that a person may do when he or she is supposed to be listening to you in a one-to-one conversation. Mark an S next to those that you usually consider supportive of you as a listener. Mark an X next to those that tell you the person is not paying attention to you. Then share your answers in a small group. You may be surprised by how different people interpret nonverbal signals.

looking at watch	looking down
doodling with a pencil	frowning, smiling
twisting a strand of hair	drumming fingers
looking you in the eye	looking at your face but not your eyes
twisting a ring	fiddling with an object (pen, coins)
leaning toward you	nodding

Were there any surprises? If your classmates have lived in foreign countries, did they provide any examples of different behaviors?

→ *See Listening Practice 4, page 99 for further material.*

Exchanging Information

An important part of communication is giving and getting information. Many people take this skill for granted but then find themselves with problems at home, on their jobs, or in school, because they did not present their information carefully or listen carefully for information they needed. Or they did not ask the right questions to find out what they needed to know. We listen most frequently to understand what another person is trying to tell us. But because we do this type of listening so often we may not work as hard at it as we should.

Listening to understand is the basis for the other types of listening. Unless you understand a message accurately, you cannot analyze the other person's ideas or respond to the other person's feelings. Consider this by thinking about the following questions:

1. Can you follow an accurate set of oral directions for getting somewhere such as a movie theater or for baking something such as a pie?

2. How well can you take orders in person or over the telephone and follow them as the speaker wished?

3. How well do you take organized notes in class that contain the important points of what the teacher said?

Listening Lab

1. Have a friend give you the following food order as if you worked in a restaurant. When your friend is done, repeat the order accurately, or ask questions to make your information accurate.

"I would like
1 roast beef on rye, hold the mayo
1 ham and swiss on whole wheat
1 tuna salad on wheat toast
2 large orders of fries
2 orange drinks
1 diet cola
Oh, and an order of your onion rings.
This is to go."

2. Assume you are in a theatre class or stage makeup course and listening to the following lecture. One person should read the lecture notes and another should answer the questions at the end.

"Today we will discuss the kinds of makeup. Makeup materials are divided into powder, paint and applicators. Let's talk about paint first. Paint may be grease or greaseless and comes in tubes, sticks and in liquid form. It includes base skin colors and special shades for creating shadows or highlights. It serves as the basic makeup. Powder is used after the paint. It will set the makeup, soften it, or prevent it from smearing. It can also tone down the paint under the lights. Applicators are brushes, pencils, powder puffs, and cleansing tissues. They help you put on or remove the makeup.

"Makeup artists have to read the script carefully and decide what kinds of characters are needed. Age, temperament, ethnic/racial characteristics, health, sex, and even mood will influence the makeup artist's decision about what to choose. When applying makeup you may have to change the person's face very dramatically or you may just need to highlight certain features slightly."

1. What are the three types of makeup materials?

2. Why is powder used after the paint?

3. What are four things about a character a makeup artist will take into consideration when planning makeup for an actor?

→ See Listening Practice 5, page 100 for further material.

Exerting Control

Everyone needs to be able to engage in different types of controlling communication, or communication that involves persuasion. You need to be able to present information persuasively, to argue and negotiate with other people, and to give and take orders. From a listening perspective, it is very important that you can analyze persuasive messages directed at you so that you can make careful judgment about how to respond. You may need to question or argue with the speaker. In short, you need to be able to take control of your response.

The mind of an analyzing listener is always busy, sorting out points, looking for good ideas and for problems. This listener hears the other person's ideas first and then figures out how to respond effectively. Consider this by thinking about the following questions:

1. How well do you hold your own in an argument?

2. How well do you catch mistakes in reasoning while you listen?

3. How easy is it to persuade you to do something when the speaker plays on your emotions?

4. How are you likely to respond to a speaker if you disagree with his or her idea or you think you have a better idea?

Listening Lab

1. Have someone read you the following statement that might be read as a radio public service announcement. As a thoughtful listener, what questions would you raise? How would you respond to the appeal?

"Volunteers are needed to work at the Family Cancer Support Center located in the Richmond Community House. Approximately 200 people participate in these programs, which include social events, telephone support; pen pals; hospital, home, and school visits; and bimonthly support meetings.

"The meetings are held for four different groups: parents, children, young adults, and siblings. The response to the program has been greater than expected. Volunteers of all ages are needed. Many types of work are available.

"Call 822-4506 if you are interested and have some time to share."

2. Have someone read you the following persuasive appeals. What techniques do the persuaders seem to be using to get you to do what they want or to believe what they say?

"All the beautiful people wear Butler jeans."

"Herman's Ketchup is the favorite of the Seattle Seahawks."

"Nine out of ten doctors recommend aspirin-free Pendalsun for those tension headaches."
→ *See Listening practice 6, page 101 for further materials.*

Sharing Feelings

Sharing feelings requires personal effort and risk for both speaker and listener. Often people become uncomfortable when a conversation moves into discussing feelings, because they do not know how to respond to a person who is talking about his or her feelings. Yet very often a person who is talking about his or her feelings just needs someone to listen . And sometimes a nonverbal response such as a look or a touch is what is needed. Consider this by thinking about the following questions:

1. How comfortable are you when another person expresses anger at something you said or did?

2. How do you feel inside when another person really shares strong feelings about sensitive subjects such as death, family problems, or health fears?

3. How often do you find yourself switching the topic or trying to cheer up someone who is sad because you are uncomfortable listening to their heavy feelings?

Listening Lab

1. Someone should read the following short statements out loud. Then tell how you think your friend would be feeling if he or she were the speaker and, secondly, what you might say in response to such a comment.

A. "I'm really worried. My mom went into the hospital for tests last week and now when I ask her about them she just says, "We have to wait and see." She and my father are acting really strange—very tense—but they won't tell me what is going on."

B. "I can't believe it. I've always wanted a summer job singing at Six Flags, but I never thought I'd really get one. It was just a big dream. And here this director tells me he really wants me! I can't stand it! This is the dream come true. Ever since I was 10 and saw the show, I wanted to be up there. And this summer the little kids are going to be looking at me."

C. "My boss is such a jerk. He tells me to take charge of training the four new waitresses and then every time he sees them do anything, he corrects them. I'm trying to teach them the most important stuff first, and he yells at them about all kinds of little stuff. If he wants me to do the job, he should let me do it."

→ *See Listening Practice 7, page 101 for further material.*

Enjoying Yourself

When you think about listening for pleasure, you may immediately think of listening to something musical. Most people find a great deal of their listening pleasure comes from music. But often you listen to other people's speech for pleasure. It may be your father telling his corny old jokes, your grandmother telling her stories of the old country, or your friends playing verbal games. It may also include your favorite radio personalities chatting, friends reciting their own poetry, or the community theater putting on a production. Although you need the same listening skills that you need for any other listening situation, your mind-set may be different if you are listening for enjoyment. You may be more relaxed in this situation. Consider this by answering the following questions:

1. In what situations do you find yourself listening for pleasure?

2. How carefully do you concentrate when you see that a situation involves listening for pleasure?

3. What is a favorite topic for you to talk about, one in which half the pleasure is just discussing this with another person (for example, sports, music, dating, hobbies)?

4. Whom do you enjoy listening to for fun? Why?

Listening Lab

1. Have someone read the following statement. Try to remember and repeat similar statements that combine silliness and sense.

"Once upon a time there were four people named Everybody, Somebody, Nobody and Anybody. When there was an important job to be done, Everybody was sure that Somebody would do it. Anybody could have done it, but Nobody did it.

"When Nobody did it, Everybody got angry because it was Everybody's job. Everybody thought that Somebody would do it, but Nobody realized that Nobody would do it.

"So it ended up that Everybody blamed Somebody when Nobody did what Anybody could have done in the first place."

2. Listen very carefully to the speech of someone whom you really enjoy listening to. Try to figure out what makes this person so funny or enjoyable. Is it a choice of words, a use of pauses, a set of stories? Try to imitate a minute of the person's speech and share it with the class.

→ *See Listening Practice 8, on page 102 for more material.*

Listening and Your Life

How useful is listening anyway? How does it really affect your life? When you really stop to think about it, you will find that you spend a great deal of time each day listening. Listening experts Florence Wolff and her associates estimate that 75 percent of our daily communication is oral and requires us to be articulate speakers and efficient listeners. We listen more than we speak, or read, or write. Effective listening is a survival skill.

Listening affects every part of our life. As a family member your ability to listen has a great effect on the quality of communication in your home, marriage, and family. Counselors report that some of the greatest difficulties in family life come from poor listening habits. Family members may start to take each other for granted and presume they know what other family members think. A husband assumes he knows what his wife thinks and, therefore, he does not listen to what she actually says. A young woman presumes she knows what her parents will say and will not listen to what they do say. Everyone can cite examples of communication breakdowns in families because people did not really listen to each other.

Listening also affects your school life. As a student you will spend between 53 and 90 percent of your time in class listening to the teacher or to other students depending on the course and your year in school. Research tells us that most teachers talk two-thirds of the time. You know what that means you are supposed to be doing! Even on breaks from classes, you spend time listening to your friends. You might be shocked to figure out just how many hours a year you spend listening in school.

Finally, listening skills are critical in the world of work. The business community views listening as one of the top ten skills necessary for good employee performance. A recent study by John Muchmore and Kathleen Galvin tried to identify the communication skills needed by new workers on a job after graduation from community college. Employers in a variety of areas such as health, business, engineering and public service were asked to rate the importance of communication skills. The skill receiving the highest rating was a listening skill—"understanding directions." In general, the listening skills received the highest ratings from employers in the field.

Often we don't think about how listening is part of almost every job. The following statements describe how listening skills affect the work life of two people in very different careers.

Manager, Bridal Salon:

"I have to really listen to find out what each girl wants. I try to find out what kind of reception she's having, how many guests will be there. If it's a small family wedding in the back yard, you pick one type of gown. If it's at the Ritz-Carlton in the evening with 500 guests, you have to find something really elaborate and different. If the reception's in a church basement, you don't want a train that goes across the whole room. But I also want to know what she has pictured in her mind, how she wants to look. Every little girl has had a dream of her wedding, and if she can tell me about it, I can usually help her choose a gown she'll love."

Chicago Tribune

Airport Customs Inspector:

"Being on the bag line is like playing mental chess with the passengers. You'll throw out some questions, you'll get their responses. Sometimes their responses don't add up. You'll ask a person, 'How long have you been abroad?' Of course you'll have that answer in front of you on the passport. And they'll say, 'Three days.' And you say, 'Business or pleasure?' 'Uh, pleasure.' 'Well, how come only three days? You spent $1000 on a ticket?' 'Well, I had a death in the family.' And then you'll check their ticket, and it was bought three months ago, and it was the same return flight, so there wasn't any change. That ought to alert you that something is going on."

Chicago Tribune

Look at the following list of career opportunities and try to imagine one in which listening skills would *not* be a basic job requirement: postal worker, flight attendant, accountant, travel agent, truck driver, gas station attendant, store manager, salesperson, teacher, welder, driving instructor, lawyer, machine operator, resort manager, insurance agent, farmer, actor, reporter.

Almost every type of work requires some type of listening skill. If you are employed, you are likely to spend a large amount of time each day listening to co-workers, bosses, customers, or the general public.

Listening Lab

1. Think about listening in families. You may use your own family, a friend's family, or a family from literature or television. Describe a situation that became a problem because certain family members did not listen to each other. How did the problem get resolved?

2. In your journal keep a log of your communication activites during a typical three hours in a classroom. Every five minutes indicate how you have been spending your time. Code your communication as listening (L), speaking (S), writing (W), and reading (R). Tally it up and get a sense of how much of the time is spent doing each. Share these findings with a small group of classmates.

3. Ask three friends who are employed to complete the sentence, "Listening is important to my work because _____." As a group, combine the responses and create a list of reasons for using listening skills in the world of work.

Listening Inventory

Take a minute to think about your current listening skills. What are your strong points? What skills would you like to improve? Use the following set of questions to begin that thinking process.

1. I am most satisfied with my listening skill in the following situation(s): _____.

2. I am least satisfied with my listening skill in the following situations(s): _____.

3. I have to work very hard when I listen to _____.

4. I enjoy relaxing and listening to _____.

5. I wish I were a better listener in the following situation(s): _____.

6. The type of speaker comments that turn me off immediately are _____.

7. The type of speaker comments that keep me interested are _____.

8. The nonverbal speaker characteristics that make a person easy for me to listen to are _____.

9. The nonverbal speaker characteristics that make a person hard for me to listen to are _____.

10. I listen to get basic information in the following situations(s): _____.

11. I listen to analyze the speaker's message in the following situation(s): _____.

12. I am willing to respond to a speaker with questions when _____.

13. I am not willing to respond to a speaker with questions when _____.

14. I believe I could be a better listener if I _____.

15. One personal goal I have in the area of listening is _____.

In this chapter we have looked at: (1) the process of communication, (2) the process of listening, (3) the purposes for listening, (4) the ways listening affects your life.

In the next chapters we will show you how to develop your listening skills. As you read the following chapters, remember: *Effective listening is a survival skill!*

"I know you believe you understand what you think I said, but I am not sure you realize that what you heard is not what I meant."

Anonymous

CHAPTER

2

GETTING THE MEANING

The Perception Process

The Context

Barriers to Listening

Introduction

Many times when we act as listeners, we find that we didn't really get the message. We looked at the speaker, we heard the speaker's voice, but we missed the point. Such communication breakdowns show us that effective listening can be difficult.

Before you begin the study of meaning and listening, let's see how you might deal with the following situations. Read the following examples and figure out why each of them could lead to misunderstandings.

□ A friend says to you, "I'll meet you at our favorite restaurant at 9."

□ You are listening in class on a spring day and three bumblebees fly in the window.

□ The luncheon chairman says, "Stop at the store on your way over and pick up some baklava and three stollen."

□ Your friend grumbles, "Yeah, I'd love to go shopping with you."

□ You are in a noisy restaurant trying to listen to the waiter recite the luncheon specials, but you have a bad cold and your ears are partly blocked.

□ You play a guessing game and are challenged to identify the following creature: "It is small with a long nose, ears, and tail, the latter being naked and prehensile. The opposable first hind toe is clawless, and the tip is expanded into a flat pad. The other digits all bear claws. The best known species is about the size of a cat, gray in color, the fur being wooly."

□ You try to listen to a guest speaker in class who is wearing dangling earrings, four shiny bracelets on each arm, and many metal necklaces.

□ You are on a committee to help resettle refugee families. You are to take two young people shopping for clothes. When they meet you, they are carrying a note that says the interpreter who was to go along is ill.

Confusion could arise in each of these situations because you may not be getting the message as the speakers intend them. Everyone experiences some communication breakdowns, no matter how hard he or she tries to be a careful listener. Yet, you can reduce the number of missed messages and misunderstandings.

In the following pages, we will look at: (1) the perception process, (2) clues in the context (3) barriers to listening.

The Perception Process

Perception is the process by which you filter and interpret what your senses tell you, so you can create a meaningful picture of the world. The perception process involves two steps:

1. Something affects your senses; you see, hear, taste, smell, or touch something.

2. You interpret the sensation. You assign meaning to what you are seeing, hearing, tasting, smelling, or touching.

For example, you hear a child say, "I don't feel good;" you see her sad face; you feel her hot head and assign the meaning, "She is sick with a fever." Or, you may hear a friend say loudly, "It's about time you showed up;" seeing his tight mouth and wrinkled forehead, and you assign the meaning, "He is angry." Yet, not every person assigns the same meaning to the same sense messages. As a listener, you need to be aware of how the perception process can influence your ability to understand a message.

___

Differences in Perception

People may perceive the same sense message differently for many reasons. Three major factors that influence perception are:

1. physical differences
2. past experiences, general and unique
3. present feelings or circumstances

Physical Differences

Although most of us have the use of all our senses, we do not have exactly the same abilities. For example, you might be farsighted, but your brother is nearsighted. Therefore, as you sit together in the back of a large auditorium and listen to a graduation speaker, you can see her facial expressions and hand movements more easily than your brother can. If you have a bad cold and your brother does not, he may be able to hear the speaker's words more easily. If your sister who is graduating sits on the stage behind the speaker, she might realize how nervous the speaker is from the fact that her knees shake; but you cannot see that from the back of the audience. After the speech, the three of you might each have a slightly different version of the presentation. Such physical differences may reflect a temporary or permanent change in your ability to take in sense data compared to someone else.

Past Experiences

Our past experiences contribute actively to our differences in perception and to our ability to understand what we are hearing. Past experiences may range from those that are considered general, or shared by many people you know, to those that are unique, or shared by few people you know. For example, if you grew up in a large Italian community, you and your community friends may easily understand expressions such as "al dente" or "Saint Joseph's Table Celebration." Other friends may need a careful explanation.

Our past experience will influence how we accept or reject a message. Suppose you have spent time volunteering at a local soup kitchen. If your state senator says, "We do not have hungry people in our district;" you are likely to reject the message.

Past experiences sometimes allow us to listen carefully and to understand words, nonverbal messages, or experiences. If the speaker talks about a subject that is not part of our past experience, we have to work harder to understand the message. In some cases, we will not be able to understand part of, or even most of, the message.

Present Feelings and Circumstances

Our current state has some effect on how we perceive a message. Our emotions, health, and various concerns are factors in how we listen. For example, if you are really upset about a fight you had with your boss, a joke that seemed funny last week would not get a laugh from you today. A headache, rumbling stomach, or sore muscles may keep you from listening carefully. If you are going on a job interview tomorrow, a lecture on how to interview will definitely hold your attention. The person sitting next to you, who has held the same job for two years, may fall asleep.

Every listener needs to be aware of the perception process. You need to know how your physical state, past experiences, and your current feelings and circumstances affect the way you listen.

Listening Lab

1. Think about your own background, and select words or terms that are part of your personal heritage that a listener from a different background might have difficulty interpreting. These terms may reflect your ethnic, religious, regional, or family heritage. They may also reflect your interests, hobbies, or work experiences. Put the word or term in a context by using it in a sentence. See how many listeners can figure out the meaning. Read and interpret the examples; then do your own.

"Every summer, my family goes *spelunking* along the bluffs of the Mississippi River. We also collect fossils."

"My father keeps his old *shillelagh* over the fireplace. It's a reminder of his years of walking through the hills of Ireland as a young man."

My brother and sister-in-law are so good at *clogging* that they perform in many regional fairs and have won many contests.

→ *See Listening Practice 9, page 102 for explanations.*

2. Set up a class situation to demonstrate physical differences in perception related to sight. For example, three or four students should stand in a line. Another person stands at a distance from them and sends nonverbal messages, using gestures and facial expressions. Each person in line should write down his or her interpretation and then read it aloud. Then, move the sender further away from the line of people. Have the sender do another message. The listeners should again write and report. Keep backing up the sender until there are conflicting reports from the listeners in line because some cannot see the nonverbal clues clearly.

3. Four volunteers are needed. Three leave the room, with the understanding that they will be asked to listen to a newspaper story and then to tell it to another person. Someone should select a newspaper story → *see Listening Practice 10, page 102,* and read it to the first volunteer. Then ask volunteer 2 to come in and listen while volunteer 1 recounts the story as accurately as possible. Volunteer 3 comes in and listens to volunteer 2's version. Continue until the last volunteer repeats the story to the whole class. It is valuable for each class member to take notes on the following: (1) information that was omitted as the story was passed on, (2) any new information that was introduced which was not in the original story, and (3) whether any volunteer changed the emphasis on what was important in the story. In a discussion afterwards, try to analyze why certain information was included and why other parts were dropped. Discuss the similarities between the first and last versions of the story.

The Context

Good listeners are like good detectives. They put pieces of a puzzle together to get the whole story. Sometimes, a speaker's message contains the whole story, but often you are left feeling something is missing. There is more to the message than meets the eye—or the ear!

All verbal messages occur within a context. By context we mean the background of a message that throws light on the meaning of the words. The context provides clues for interpreting the words accurately. Effective listeners read the clues and try to understand the background to find the very best possible interpretations of a message. In short, they try to put the message *in context*.

For example, you may hear your coach yelling at a visiting player, "Don't you come back here unless you can respect our equipment." The visitor may say, "Wow, he's really mean. He could have asked politely." You may say, "He's not usually like that. His daughter just had eye surgery and he's been very tense." Or you may say, "Last year he had to replace $50.00 worth of equipment after the Maryville game. He's just being careful." You are adding data, or puzzle pieces, to try to explain the context of the coach's message.

To place a message in context, you may need to think about: (1) the person, (2) the setting, (3) the occasion, and (4) the verbal/nonverbal connection. Knowing something about these four factors will help you solve some puzzles. Let's look at each of these areas.

The Person

Often you hear expressions such as, "Oh, don't mind Art. His bark is worse than his bite." Only someone who has known Art for a while could say this. When you know people well, you are more likely to interpret their messages accurately. You may be able to predict their reactions. Therefore, when they say something, you may think to yourself. . .

☐ "Alice really likes that idea. She's just shy and doesn't express her feelings very quickly."

☐ "Mrs. Decker always says 'No' first to any proposal for change. She eventually comes around."

Although you might be wrong on occasion, usually your knowledge of the speaker as a person helps you to be an accurate listener.

Knowing about the recent events in a person's life may explain why he or she says something in a particular way. Remember the example of the coach whose daughter had surgery? You may find that you will listen to a person differently if you realize that he or she recently:

• failed a final exam

• had a serious operation

In addition, knowledge of a person's history can also add to your listening effectiveness. For example, you may be more sensitive to comments made about cancer surgery, if you knew that person had had such surgery four years ago. The more a listener knows about a speaker, the easier it is to put the speaker's remarks *in context*. This results in more accurate listening.

→ *See Listening Practice 11, page 103 for more on personal context.*

The Setting

Effective listeners consider place and time when interpreting a message. A person may feel free to talk in one place and not in another, or to say something at one time and not at another. Let's look at the issue of place first.

You may interpret what someone says differently if:

☐ you are seated in a crowded restaurant where your conversation can be easily heard. You wonder if your friend is being as open as she would be in a private place.

□ you are with a small group of people and one close friend of yours is talking vaguely about a problem. You may wonder if she would be more direct if you were alone with her.

The size, privacy, and comfort of a place may affect a speaker's message as well as the listener's effectiveness in hearing it.

In the same way, time may influence a message. You may find yourself thinking:

□ "Time was running out, so that's why she stopped talking so abruptly."

□ "Mark usually gets grumpy when it's late and he's tired."

□ "Jeff was only going to be in town for a day, so why should he raise sore subjects in that short time?"

The time of day, or the amount of time available, often influence what someone says, or how someone says it. The careful listener may need to consider the issue of time when placing a message in context. In short, good listeners check how the setting, place, and time influence the message.

The Occasion

Sometimes an occasion or an event calls for certain types of communication. Perhaps when you were a child, your parents said, "Don't fuss and spoil Grandma's birthday." Or, "It's Emmy's graduation, so be nice to Uncle Henry." In the same way, a formal speech is usually tailored to an occasion. For example, you may hear comments such as:

□ "Martha had to say nice things about her experience in Colombia. She was speaking at the exchange students' banquet."

□ "Of course, he watched his jokes to be sure they were suitable for families. That cable show was the big fund-raising kickoff."

People also tailor their conversation to certain occasions. A speaker should be careful in choosing words and may be formal in manner when attending a funeral or going on a job interview. Yet at a football game or a party, the same speaker may use lots of slang, a loud voice, and very broad gestures and tell a lot of jokes. If you only saw the person in one of these types of settings, you would only have one image from which to interpret his or her messages. Yet, you might think, "I'll bet that person might be different in another situation." As a listener, you need to ask yourself, "How might the occasion be affecting this person's speech?"

The Verbal/Nonverbal Connection

Think of the many meanings that you could give to the short sentence, "I will send the flowers." Depending on which word gets the emphasis, some of the possibilities are:

□ *"I"* (not you).

□ "...*will*..." (no, I didn't do it yet).

□ "...*send*..." (not deliver them).

□ "...*flowers*—" (you bring the candy).

A listener depends on nonverbal cues in order to interpret even that short simple sentence accurately. The speaker's vocal tone, gestures, facial expression, and movements would probably tell you about the intent of the message. Although words are a valuable source of meaning, the nonverbal cues that accompany the words help to put them *in context.*

There is a strong relationship between verbal and nonverbal parts of a message. Nonverbal communication may (1) support, (2) highlight, (3) replace, (4) contradict or (5) regulate verbal communication.

Nonverbal messages usually *support* verbal messages. The words and facial expressions, vocal tones, or movements seem consistent with each other. For example, people who are serious about a message do not laugh; rather, they may look directly at you and refrain from smiling. People who are excited and happy usually demonstrate this through an excited tone of voice, a cheerful facial expression, and wide movements. Most listeners expect similarity between a speaker's verbal and nonverbal messages. If this is missing, the listener starts to pay greater attention to what is going on, looking for clues about any possible difficulties. Consistent messages may clarify or repeat a message, but still they appear natural and comfortable.

When a speaker uses nonverbal communication to call attention to part of their message, it may be a way of *highlighting* the point or saying, ''This is very important.'' When a speaker holds up three fingers to signify three points, pounds on the table, and changes tone of voice dramatically, the message may be: Pay attention. Effective listeners are alert for nonverbal messages telling them what is important.

On occasion, nonverbal messages *replace* verbal ones entirely. Usually this occurs with short responses such as nodding to answer a question or using a hand signal for greetings or directions. People at a distance may greet each other with a wave rather than a comment. Effective listeners must be able to decode the facial expressions or gestures or movements if verbal clues are not available.

Although it does not happen frequently, there are times when someone's nonverbal clues will *contradict* what the person is saying verbally. This is often referred to as the ''mixed message.'' For example, you frown and say you are happy; you walk slowly while complaining you are very late. As a listener, you learn to see mixed messages as warnings that you had better pay close attention. You may even need to discuss the contradiction. A good listener may respond, ''You say you like the idea, but you don't look very enthusiastic about it.'' Or, ''You say there's no rush, but you keep looking at your watch. What is really going on?'' Effective listeners watch carefully for mixed messages.

Finally one person's nonverbal messages may *regulate* the flow of another's verbal messages. If you as a listener appear to be bored, the speaker may talk faster to finish up or stop abruptly. If you appear friendly, relaxed, and interested, the speaker may put in more examples and tell you more information. If you look confused, the speaker may stop and ask for questions or restate the last point. Your nonverbal messages guide the speaker's verbal responses.

By now it should be very clear that listeners must be aware of the verbal/nonverbal connection. Remember, nonverbal communication may: (1) support, (2) highlight, (3) replace, (4) contradict, or (5) regulate verbal communication.

Listening Lab

1. Describe an actual incident when you had to explain to a third party what someone close to you really meant to say. Explain what the person close to you (e.g., friend or family member) usually sounds like and how his or her communication was different in this incident. Exactly what explanation did you give?

2. From a listener's perspective, explain how the following circumstances could affect the way a person would talk about one of the following topics: a) money, b) health, c) friendship.

• speaker just lost a good job

• speaker's mother has diabetes

• speaker trained hard and ran a successful marathon

• speaker has just moved from the community where he or she was raised

3. Read the following sentences to the class emphasizing different words each time. Discuss interpretation of the meaning as the emphasis changes.

a.) "Put the tape on the desk."
put (don't toss)
tape (not the scissors)
on (not inside)
desk (not the windowsill)

b.) "I should buy her three new dresses?"
I (me? not you?)
should (maybe if I want to)
buy (sew her two of them maybe)
her (why not her sister)
three (she'll be lucky to get one)
new (she just got new clothes last week)
dresses (she almost never wears dresses)

4. Explain how time affects your listening ability. Describe how the time of day can interfere with your ability to be an effective listener.

5. As a listener, list the verbal and nonverbal clues that tell you the speaker is feeling pressured to finish talking quickly in three of these situations:

• teacher is completing a history course this week

• employer is hurrying to meet a client

• newscaster is trying to break for a commercial

7. List some of the rules you were given as a child for speaking and listening at family events when your relatives would be in attendance.

8. How might the following occasions affect the verbal and/or nonverbal aspects of a person's speech? Think of what is said, and how it is said.

• a rehearsal dinner before a wedding

• a rock concert out of doors

• a production of *Julius Caesar*

• a swim club year-end banquet

9. Have someone read "When You Lose Your Wallet" (→ *Listening Practice 12, page 103*) with very few gestures using a monotone. Have people list the points made. Then have it read again, asking the speaker to highlight nonverbally the main points. Have people list the points made. Compare the listening effectiveness of class members when nonverbals were not effective and when they were used to highlight the information.

10. Have someone read the following sentences either of two ways: (1) let the verbal and nonverbal messages support each other; or (2) have the nonverbal message contradict the verbal one. See if you can tell which way the sentence is being read.

☐ "I really like that dress."

☐ "I can't wait until school starts again."

☐ "I'm sure Gary would be able to fix it for you."

→ *See Listening Practice 13, page 103, for more sentences.*

11. Set up a two person role play in which one person is expected to insert a totally nonverbal message (replacing the verbal) into the conversation. The listener should be able to understand and continue or comply with the command without asking for a verbal explanation. → *See Listening Practice 14, page 103,* for the nonverbal messages to insert into the verbal conversation.

12. As a listener, give an unsuspecting speaker nonverbal feedback intended to regulate his or her presentation. Record the results in your journal or share them with the class. For example, when a friend starts to tell you about a recent vacation, give that person positive nonverbal feedback: smile, nod your head, and keep strong eye contact. See what happens.

Barriers to Listening

All listeners discover certain barriers that keep them from listening effectively. Each of us can remember times when someone was talking and suddenly we realized we had no idea what was being said. We simply tuned out. Or can you recall having a conversation with someone and two minutes later not remembering a word? All you know is that a jet plane went by or loud music distracted you.

There are seven common barriers to good listening. They are: (1) external distractions, (2) internal distractions, (3) conflicting demands, (4) speaker's credibility, (5) speaker's style, (6) your lack of information, (7) your personal biases, (8) your desire to talk. In this section, you will learn how the barriers work and how you can begin to overcome them.

External Distractions

External distractions refer to situations in the environment that keep you from paying careful attention to the speaker. Such distractions may include a spider climbing up the wall in front of you, the garbage truck churning outside, or the ringing of the telephone. Everyone knows how hard it is to carry on a conversation when a small child wants your attention or when the family dog is jumping all over you.

Some external distractions are temporary and unusual. But sometimes, the external distractions are long-term or permanent. You may go to school near a busy airport, or the train may run by your house every half-hour. You may live with noisy children. Sometimes you can change the distractions by shutting the windows or going to another place. Other times you have to learn to listen in spite of them.

Good listeners try to foresee the predictable distractions and decide to ignore them. They are confused by surprise distractions at first but then work to focus on the speaker again.

Internal Distractions

Sometimes you will find that your worries or your excitement over an upcoming event will distract you from listening. If you just had an argument with a good friend or your father is very ill, you may not be able to pay close attention in class or at work. Good things, such as next weekend's camping trip or an upcoming party, may distract you from paying attention to a conversation or a lecture. Sometimes you may find yourself daydreaming instead of paying attention to what is going on around you.

As we noted earlier, your physical state may interfere with your ability to give full attention to someone else. Headaches, toothaches, stomach cramps, or exhaustion serve as internal distractions. If you are in pain, will you be able to give full attention to a friend's problem?

Good listeners tend to know what might distract them, so they will be prepared. If you know that you tend to daydream about your weekend plans during class, you may need to say to yourself, "I will not think about the trip until later because I need to pay attention to my teacher." If you always get hungry during a class that starts at noon, you might plan to have a snack before class starts.

Conflicting Demands

You have probably seen television commercials with a busy mother who is trying to talk on the phone, stir the soup, feed the baby, and braid the ten year old's hair. This is a classic situation with conflicting demands!

All of us get into these situations. There are times when you are trying to do too many things at once, so you cannot listen. Perhaps once or twice you appeared to listen in English class while you tried to finish your math homework. Or you tried to listen to your mother's problems while watching your favorite television show. Sometimes we find ourselves in the same situations over and over again. You may doodle, plan a meal, mentally pack a suitcase for the weekend, or count money in your head while appearing to listen carefully and well. Sometimes you are the only one who knows that you didn't get the message.

Some people are good jugglers. They can talk to one person on the phone and one in the room and still get most of the message. Most people can't do that. Sometimes too many conflicting demands make you feel tense, angry, and tired. You feel torn in three or four directions and nothing is done well. Each listener needs to learn personal limits.

Good listeners first become aware of the times they are most likely to experience conflicting demands. Then they try to keep those situations from arising, for example, by asking someone to call back after dinner rather than trying to talk and cook at the same time. Or they try to catch themselves at a habit like doodling and stop the behavior once it is recognized.

The Speaker's Credibility

Credibility refers to how believable the speaker is to you. A speaker with low credibility may create barriers to your listening. Which of the following persons would you believe if they tried to convince you not to start smoking? Rank them in order of the most believable (1) to the least believable (5).

• your best friend who does not smoke

• a sloppily dressed stranger on the bus

• your family doctor

• your father who smokes

• a cigarette salesperson

Some of these people might create a barrier to listening on this topic. For example, if you see someone smoking or selling cigarettes, this would be a barrier to believing the person's message about not smoking. You may tend to reject the sloppy stranger, thinking, "What does he know?" It's hard to accept a "Do as I say, not as I do" message, especially from your parents. On the other hand, you may listen to your best friends because they don't smoke and they do care about you. The doctor's medical knowledge may also persuade you to consider the dangers of smoking seriously.

What makes people believable when they are talking to you? In some cases, a person's formal or informal reputation precedes a message. A speaker may be introduced like this: "Dr. May Jonas, Family Coordinator for Glenwood Hospital's Alcohol Program, who will talk on Al-Anon, a self-help group for teenagers." Or a reputation may be well-known: "Henry 'The Fonz' Winkler will address the school next Monday evening at 7:30. He will talk about making television sitcoms." Each of these speakers would appear to be a credible source for the specific topics.

Informal reputations often serve to influence believability. You may think of someone as a racist, liberal, burnout, or brain. Such labels tend to influence how you react to what they say.

Sometimes the speaker establishes credibility during a conversation or speech. Comments such as, "When I ran the marathon. . ." or "When I play the saxaphone. . ." indicate some knowledge of the area. When you hear two people trade baseball statistics or computer jargon for half an hour, you begin to see them as credible sources on the subject. But people who spout off on topics they don't know much about tend to create a barrier between themselves and their listeners.

The Speaker's Style

Another person's style may create listening barriers within you. Style refers to the speaker's appearance, manner of speaking, and ability to relate to the listener. A bizarre or inappropriate appearance may interfere with the message. If you are distracted by a speaker's clothes, jewelry, or hairstyle, you may miss the main point of the conversation.

Nervous mannerisms tend to distract the listener. People who constantly say "you know," who look at the floor, or who drum their fingers during a conversation invite the listener to focus on the mannerism rather than on the content.

Finally, a speaker who cannot relate directly to the listeners creates barriers. Speakers who seem harsh and prejudiced cause listeners to turn off. A speaker says, "People with money hang-ups really bug me." You may not hear the rest of what is said because you are thinking, "Me? Does he mean me? What did I say about money lately?"

Some listeners have come to know what bothers them and to overcome these barriers. You may learn not to be put off at once by someone who appears to brag. You may learn to look beyond the other person's clothes very quickly. You may question the speaker who is too technical.

Good listeners can sometimes remember occasions when they judged someone too quickly and later discovered how much they had missed. Usually these listeners resolve to keep an open mind the next time.

Your Lack of Information

Sometimes you will find that no matter how hard you try to listen, you cannot interpret what the speaker is saying. Your past experiences do not give you the background for understanding the verbal or nonverbal clues. Your general and unique past experiences give you a working vocabulary with which to interpret meanings. If the person you are talking with does not use verbal and nonverbal symbols you are familiar with, you are in trouble as a listener.

An obvious example arises when people come from a culture we have not experienced. Their language and use of gestures is different from ours. For example, if you meet a German tourist who does not speak English, you may be able to figure out a few things he is saying by recognizing some similar words and watching certain gestures; but you certainly can't have a complete conversation. Yet if you studied German, or come from a German family, you may understand much of or all that he is saying.

Even when you speak a particular language, sometimes the words or gestures are so specific to a particular group that you cannot understand. Suppose your friend asked you to help out backstage at the community theater for a week. How would you interpret the stage manager's directions to you if she said, "Take the scoop up and attach it to the batten. Take the scoop by the yoke and slide the clamp over the batten until the pipe is securely inside the C. With your other hand, tighten the clamp screw until the clamp is securely fastened to the batten. Use the wrench." Unless you are familiar with stage lighting, good luck! No matter how hard you listen, you won't be able to follow the directions on the first try.

Good listeners take the risk of asking questions to find out what they cannot understand. They will also try to learn to interpret new words and nonverbal symbols in order to be more effective in the future. Sometimes—though it is not easy—you may have to say, "I don't understand now, but I'll try to learn more about it."

Your Personal Biases

Personal biases may keep you from really hearing what another person has to say. We all have our own beliefs and attitudes on certain subjects that may reflect our research and careful thoughts on the topic. Yet many people believe they have heard all that can be said on one side of a subject. Some people see only what they wish to see and hear only what they wish to hear. This leads to closed minds and creates barriers to communication.

Sometimes you create a barrier just because you believe a subject is uninteresting. Which of the following subjects is likely to cause you to close down mentally?

• the U.S. Space Camp for teenagers

• the benefits of vegetarian diets

• investing in stocks

• losing weight safely

• trends in rock music

Some of the above topics may meet with a "ho-hum" from you. Yet many of these are very interesting topics if discussed with an interested audience.

Sensitive topics may cause barriers to good listening. Each of us has strong feelings about discussing values with anyone, but particularly with people we don't know well. If a person you just met started to ask you about your religion, that may set up a barrier. But you and a trusted friend may talk for hours about your religious beliefs, and you might feel very comfortable. Some people tune out topics they think will be too technical or difficult. Their reasoning is, "I could never understand it anyway, so why should I even try?" Yet topics in areas such as agriculture, economics, science, medicine, or business can be made interesting to listeners. Also, active listeners tend to ask questions and ask for explanations and examples. Their interaction keeps the speaker aware of listener needs.

Sometimes you will tune out after hearing a speaker take a particular position, reasoning to yourself, "I hold the opposite view. Why should I bother to listen?" This often happens around national/political topics such as nuclear freeze, welfare, or government spending. But it can also happen on issues of personal taste such as sports or music or—as mentioned earlier—dress. You may learn more and more about one point of view but remain unaware of other positions or ideas.

Good listeners try to remain open to new ideas. They try to figure out why the speaker finds a topic interesting or why the speaker holds a particular point of view. By trying to listen, you may even learn something useful in the process!

Your Desire to Talk

Most people would rather talk than listen, especially if they have to listen carefully. You all know someone who may appear to be listening, but who is really sitting there waiting to talk. You can remember arguments when it was all you could do to wait for the other person to finish. Maybe you didn't wait, but you just jumped in and started making your point anyway. In these situations, very little listening is going on. You may get so excited about making your point that you interrupt the other speakers or you send nonverbal messages telling them to stop.

At other times, people compete to "top" the other person's joke or story. You can recognize this listener as the one who says, "That's nothing. Why I had to. . ." or "You think that's bad, wait till you hear this. . ." Usually, this competition takes the fun out of the conversation because the speakers in effect only talk to themselves.

People who find themselves always trying to get in the next word need to learn the value of controlling their talking. Good listeners use the active listening technique of paraphrasing the speaker's comments before responding. This technique, which we will talk more about later, really forces you to hear what the other person is saying before you think of your own points or arguments.

Every speaker and listener has the responsibility to try to reach the other. This cannot happen when barriers go up and one or both persons stop trying. It's a two-way street; both people have to make an effort.

Adlai Stevenson described this ideal well when he said, ''My assignment is to talk to you for awhile, and yours is to listen to me. I trust we will both finish our work at the same time.''

Listening Lab

1. During one hour of class, note in your journal all the external distractions that occur. Star the ones you had not been aware of during the term before, recording them in your journal. Compare what you heard or saw with the observations of other people in the class.

2. Role play a restaurant scene in which there are three tables, each with separate two- or three-person conversations going on. At each table, one student should try to keep track of the conversation in his or her group while also trying to keep track of the conversation at another table. When the entire role play is finished, the participants should describe their reactions to the experience and compare notes on what they learned at each table simultaneously. Try to answer the question: When is it possible to respond to conflicting demands effectively?

3. Create a message with at least five technical terms based on your job, hobbies, or interests. In groups of five, each person should share the message, repeating each technical term twice. Each listener gets one point for each term interpreted correctly. The listener with the highest score in each group is the winner.

4. Rate your reactions to listening to opinions on the following value-oriented topics in a conversation with friends or with casual acquaintances.

	Positive		Undecided		Negative	
	Friend	Acquaintance	Friend	Acquaintance	Friend	Acquaintance
politics						
money						
divorce						
religion						
alcoholism						
death						
nuclear war						

5. Read the following saying and explain how it applies to the listening barrier of the speaker's image: ''What you are speaks so loudly that I cannot hear what you are saying.'' Give an example of a situation to which this saying might be applied.

In this chapter we have looked at: (1) the process of perception, (2) the clues in the context, and (3) barriers to listening. It should be very clear by now that listening is a process that takes motivation and effort.

"Nature has given us one tongue, but two ears, that we may hear from others twice as much as we speak."

Epictetus

CHAPTER 3
LISTENING FOR BASIC INFORMATION

Making Things Memorable

Using Thinking Strategies

Following Directions

Introduction

Each day you find yourself in countless situations in which you are expected to *get* some very basic information. You probably will do well in some cases and miss out on important information in other cases. By *getting,* we mean understanding and being able to use information. In order to think about how well you do at getting basic information, read the following questions and mark each one T for true or F for false.

1. _____ I can be introduced to someone and forget that person's name in two minutes.

2. _____ I can hear simple directions on how to get somewhere and get confused as I actually try to follow them.

3. _____ I can sit in class taking notes and get confused about what is important to know.

4. _____ I can forget one out of four things I was supposed to buy at the grocery.

5. _____ I can watch the evening news on television and five minutes later not be able to describe the first story.

6. _____ I sometimes find myself answering a question other than the one that I was asked.

7. _____ I usually have to ask a waiter to repeat the day's specials twice when ordering in a restaurant.

8. _____ I can hear things, such as graduation requirements, repeated three times and still miss some important points.

9. _____ I can think I'm listening very hard to a speaker and suddenly discover I am daydreaming.

10. _____ I should ask more questions of a speaker in order to get all the information I need.

If you answered *true* to three or more questions, you should give special attention to this chapter. Everyone has some difficulty getting basic information. Yet with a little work the amount of information you understand and use can increase a great deal. To show you how to increase your ability to get basic information, we will look at the following areas: (1) making things memorable, (2) using thinking strategies, and (3) following directions. Finding main ideas, one of the most important listening skills, will be covered in Chapter 4.

Making Things Memorable

What gets your attention when you are listening to someone? How does a speaker get your attention back if you are beginning to daydream? What makes you sit up and take special notice even if the speaker is not very interesting? Before we get into specific kinds of basic information, let's look at the process of making things stand out for the listener.

We can use the MTM model to understand what affects you as a listener—in other words, "*M*aking *T*hings *M*emorable." Although much of the work has to be done by the speaker, the listener can be alert for what is memorable. The listener can also cause some memorable things to happen. When we examine the parts of the MTM model, we are looking at: (1) change, (2) novelty, (3) repetition, (4) application, and (5) thought speed.

Change

What makes you pay special attention to the speaker? He or she makes something different happen. Something changes. It may only be the way your name is said, or it may be a movement across a stage, or a loud voice that has become suddenly hushed. Any change will tell you—"listen up"—pay attention.

Good teachers and public speakers know how to vary a presentation. They may switch from facts to stories, put up a chart or tell a joke, gesture actively or suddenly become very quiet. The change of pace forces an audience, even a captive audience, to refocus its attention on the speaker.

Even in everyday conversation, we are aware of the changes that call attention to themselves. If your friend normally calls you "Liz" but suddenly you hear her call loudly "Elizabeth," you pay closer attention. If you meet a new person and expect to exchange the usual greetings of name, home town, and so on, you may pay closer attention when the second question to you is "Whom did you vote for in the last election?"

When you are listening to directions, a change in descriptive terms may signal you to pay attention. If someone says "Go left on Green Street, go two blocks, then take another left on Stratford for six blocks, then go right on Sandles Road and watch for a small blue sign that says Tally Lane," you will listen carefully to the description of the sign. This part of the description breaks the pattern.

As a listener in a large audience situation, you may not have too many chances to effect change—but you have some. Your feedback indicating you are pleased, bored, confused, or angry could cause a speaker to stop and ask you about your nonverbal reaction. When you ask questions, you can interrupt the predictable flow of a presentation. If you provide an example, you have shifted focus from the speaker and perhaps made the talk more interesting. In everyday conversation, you may change your usual response style such as nodding your head to a verbal comment. These changes will call attention to themselves and make the conversation more memorable.

Novelty

One can make things memorable through novelty, or the totally unexpected. Even more than change, novelty involves the unique and creative act that calls attention to itself. Such novelty must be used only once in a while, or it loses its effectiveness.

Sometimes you listen to a new speaker because you have never heard him or her before and you don't know what to expect. By the second or the fifth time you hear this person, the novelty may have worn off and you may not be paying close attention. This is the time for the speaker to use novel approaches. For example, one speaker began a talk on learning foreign languages by giving the introduction in French. Another speaker describing communication among the deaf gave part of a speech in sign language.

Novelty is unique to each situation. Someone may dress in a dramatic way, make outrageous comments, or sing in the middle of a presentation. When giving directions for cooking, Julia Child, television personality and chef, says and does outrageous things to keep the viewers' attention. Although novelty involves taking a personal risk, usually it will force listeners to pay attention.

As a listener, you can appreciate and encourage novelty, but it's hard to make it happen. Yet if people are easy to listen to because of the risks they take, you can give them feedback about how they force you to pay attention. Then, maybe they'll do it again.

Repetition

If information is repeated a number of times, you are more likely to remember it than if you only hear it once. From introductions to full-fledged political speeches, repetition sends the signal—*important!* Many famous speeches include the repetition of main points. The Rev. Martin Luther King, Jr., used the phrase "Let Freedom Ring" throughout the conclusion of his "I Have a Dream" speech.

If someone says "Put in one and one-quarter cups of sugar; remember, one and one-quarter cups," you are more likely to remember the exact measurement. If it is important for flowers to be planted in "full sunlight," repeating that fact becomes very important.

Even in introductions, repetition can help you remember someone's name. Look at the difference between these two introductions of the same person:

Introduction 1: "David Jones, I'd like you to meet Joyce Stratton. You two both love basketball."

Introduction 2: "Dave, I'd like you to meet Joyce Stratton. Joyce, this is David Jones. Joyce and you share a love of basketball."

In the second introduction, you had three chances to get the first name. A wise listener then continues the repetition process by stating, "Joyce, good to meet you." After that, you're likely to remember Joyce's name when you need to introduce her to someone else in a few minutes.

Good listeners create opportunities for repetition. They may prompt the speaker to repeat, asking, "What kind of dog did you say that was?" or "Did you say the dog is called a Bishon?" If they are good listeners asking for directions, their response might be, "Tell me that again" or "Do I turn left at Spring Grove Plaza?"

 Hearing information more than once helps fix it in your mind. Repetition serves to give you extra chances to get the information and to get it right! Ask for repetition if you need it.

Application

Application involves "making it your own." You as a listener ask and answer the questions "So what?" and "How does it relate to me?" If you can apply information to yourself, you are more likely to understand and use it.

A speaker may help you to make the application. Comments such as "You should be interested in this because of your _____" or "Since all of you are _____ you will need to know _____." Look at the following examples.

□ "Since you are graduating, it is important that you know the employment interview schedule."

□ "The photographer can't be late for the wedding. We'll start at the bride's house at 1678 Walnut at 2:30 sharp."

□ "When this bill passes in Congress, it will help families such as yours who have a child with a rare disease."

Sometimes you can apply information to yourself that the speaker does not realize has particular interest to you. How often have you listened to others talk about a diet, a method for repairing a ten-speed bike, or a lead on a job and thought to yourself—"I should know about that." You see a connection between what is said and how it applies to you.

At other times you have to work to find the connections to yourself. For example, look again at the list of possible speech topics listed in Chapter 2. Think about how each of these might apply to you and which ones might take real work to connect to your way of life in some way.

• the U.S. Space Camp for teenagers

• the benefits of vegetarian diets

• investing in stocks

• losing weight safely

• trends in rock music

Although some of those might connect to you easily, you would have to find ways to get excited about listening to some of the others.

Thought Speed

Good listeners use their thought-speed advantage in order to make things memorable. Most people speak at a rate of 120 to 180 words per minute, yet most people can listen at 400 or more words per minute. That's a big difference! Although some listeners use their extra time to daydream, plan a party or think about last week's soccer game, effective listeners put their thought-speed advantage to work. When listening to basic information, these listeners are saying to themselves, "Did I get it?" and "What can I do with it?" and "What else might I need to know?"

Listen to the following directions in the left hand column while looking at the possible thought-speed comments of a listener.

Speaker	Listener
"To get to Pam and Rick's house, you have to go up Green Bay Road until you get to Willow. Turn left on Willow. In fact, you can only go left. Take Willow out to Robindale and make a right. Then look for Elm; that's about seven blocks. At Elm, you turn left and look for Hawthorne Lane. It comes up very quickly. This is a cul-de-sac. Just circle to the right until you find 827. It's a colonial house with a bright red door. We'll see you there at 8:30."	Up? She must mean north. Oh yes, there's a bus shelter on that corner. I wonder if there are streetlights? I think Martha used to live in that area. Cul-de-sac? Oh, those little circles. Sounds right. Pam always liked Early American furniture.

When listening for basic information listeners tend to ask questions of themselves or make comments to themselves. They use the thought-speed time to be sure they understand.

Listening Lab

Think about how you can use the MTM "Making Things Memorable" model in your life. Be aware of when you can use (1) change, (2) novelty, (3) repetition, (4) application, and (5) thought speed. In order to practice using these parts of the model, try the following:

1. Have someone read the following passage a number of different ways. Try to decide which approach makes it more memorable for you. For example, the speaker may use change or novelty. Or the speaker may try to repeat key points or add statements to help you apply it to yourself.

Find a New Friend

We need 52 families to host high school exchange students from Western Europe for three weeks in April. The students will spend a six-week period in the United States—three weeks touring and three weeks attending school in this community. Most of the students speak fairly good English. They wish to live in typical American households and wish to be treated as members of the family for those three weeks. This is an unusual opportunity to share a little bit of another culture and to show American hospitality. There will be two evening events for all host families in the community to which all family members are invited. Expand your horizons. Brush up on your high school French, German, or Spanish. Sign up at City Hall to host an exchange student and find a new friend.

For another sample passage, → *see Listening Practice 15 on page 104.*

 2. Check out the effect of repetition. Six students students should volunteer. Three (Group 2) should leave the room. Then the other three (Group 1) should listen to a reading and answer questions after it. Read → *Version 1, Listening Practice 16, on page 104* to Group 1 and see if they can answer the questions after it. Read the second version to Group 2 when they come in. See how they answer the questions. As a group, compare the effect of repetition on the correctness of the answers.

3. Try to apply specific speaker's points to your own life. Listen to presentations from → *Listening Practice 17 on page 105* and make notes as you listen of what it brings to mind for you. Discuss the various ways in which people tried to apply what was heard.

4. Think of a speaker who makes things memorable to you. Get into small groups and discuss each person's choice of speaker and the techniques this person uses to make things memorable. List the similarities you find and examples of what each person does exceptionally well.

Using Thinking Strategies

How do effective listeners make sure they get the information they want? Although not all good listeners use the same methods, they all have some thinking strategies to help them get the information they need. Let's look at two examples and see how listeners might work with them. Read the following directions for grocery shopping and think about how you would remember the items. Then see how other people would listen to the list.

Directions:

"When you go to the store remember to bring home:

• a bag of white beans

• a half gallon of strawberry ice cream

• a gallon of milk

• a pound of butter

• a loaf of whole wheat bread."

How would you remember that list? Now see what three other people said about how they might remember it.

Listener 1

"The way I would go about remembering that would be to picture a hill of beans with an upside down strawberry ice cream cone melting on top into rivers of milk and butter coming down the sides. I would sit it all on a piece of bread."

Listener 2

"I would remember this by three Bs—beans, bread, butter, plus milk and ice cream."

Listener 3

"I would remember this by picturing myself walking through the grocery store where I always shop. I would picture myself walking the first aisle for milk, butter and ice cream and then going past the bakery for the bread, and finally going down a middle aisle for the beans."

Read the following introduction and imagine how you would remember the first names or something about the people. Then see what other listeners would do.

"This is Mark Miller, the magician I told you about; Sara Jameson from Portland; Paulette Hill, who lives a few blocks away; and Sarita Espinola who is organizing this bike-a-thon."

How would you remember these names? Now see how two other people said they might remember them.

Listener 1

"I would try to remember these people in different ways. I would think of the repetition of M sounds—Mark the magician. Then I would picture Portland on a map and associate it with Sara. I would probably associate a hill with Paulette. Because I never heard of Sarita before, I would think of my friend Rita and know that the name was close."

Listener 2

"I would think of M & M for Mark Miller. Sara looks like my friend Marilyn who has a sister Sara, so I would remember her by connecting her to Marilyn's sister. I would think about bicycle and hill for Paulette Hill and I would think about Esposito's grocery and Sarita together."

Let's look at five different thinking strategies people use to listen and to remember: (1) visualization, (2) association, (3) memory magic, (4) chunking, and (5) focusing. These may be used separately or in combination with each other.

Visualization

Some people learn to visualize, or create mental pictures, to help them retain information. The person who listened to the grocery list and pictured the ice cream melting on the beans was visualizing. So was the person who thought about a hill to remember Paulette Hill's name.

Read the following directions for a nature hike field trip and think about how you might visualize these things in order to remember them.

"The things you need for the field trip are a sweater, at least $4.00 for carfare and snack, your nature guidebook, a small shovel, long pants, and a hat or sunscreen if you burn easily."

People may also visualize themselves doing something related to whatever is being described. The person who visualized walking through the grocery aisles as a way of listening to the grocery list was using this technique. Read the following description of lifeguard tests and try to visualize yourself doing them as a way to remember the parts of the test.

"We make our lifeguard applicants swim 200 yards in less than 3.5 minutes, swim 20 yards underwater, dive in 16 feet of water and pick up a 20-pound bag of rocks, and break a strangle hold from one of the instructors. Then they're ready for the beaches!"

Visualization works well for some people while others find it very difficult to do. If you don't create mental pictures easily, you may find another technique more effective for you.

Association

Some listeners use the association technique. They try to create a connection between the new information or idea and something familiar. When making introductions, the speaker may help the listener associate by saying the name ("This is Charmaine") and providing information for association, ("She is Jerry's sister" or "She is a hair stylist at Vogue's"). Teachers may help you associate by saying that one assignment is similar to a past assignment.

Read the following description of duties for a summer job and imagine how you might use association to help you remember them.

"The School Board would like you to start a summer program for tutoring elementary school children. There are many first to sixth graders who need help with reading and math skills. We believe it would be valuable for you to form a group of high school or college students who would serve as successful role models and who would tutor twenty hours a week. We are able to pay the minimum wage. We will hold classes in the board room of the old library and in some of their smaller meeting rooms. The teachers will identify the possible students and will give you a list. Then you can call the parents and explain the program to them. I hope you are interested in this project."

You may find yourself associating through sounds. You may associate the name Sarita with the Spanish word "Senorita" and think of that word when you see this woman again. Or you may associate Sarita with Rita and think of that name. If you are to meet someone on Cresswell Street and you are afraid you may forget the name, you may associate it as "Cross the Well" Street. Association provides listeners with old hooks on which to hang new information.

Memory Magic

Almost everyone has played memory tricks to remember information for tests in school. Often these are very complicated schemes—but they work. In the early example of grocery shopping, one listener tried to find similar first letters while listening to the list. Out of five items that person was able to identify three B's—beans, bread and butter.

Another trick is to create new words with the first letters of each word on a list. Sometimes you have to stretch things a bit to make them fit. For example, look at the following list of groceries and imagine how you could make a word out of the first letters.

bologna

eggs

bananas

apples

potatoes

One person was able to make a word out of first initials with some slight variations of the list.

T—'taters

A—apples

B—bananas

L—lunch meat

E—eggs

Instead of initials, you can use whole words with the same initials. You may remember one such memory aid from your social science studies in elementary school. To remember the countries of Central America—*G*uatemala, *E*l Salvador, *H*onduras, *N*icaragua, *C*osta Rica, *P*anama—just remember this nonsense sentence: *G*o *e*at *h*oney *N*ancy *c*an't *p*lay.

If your teacher had lectured on the material in this section on ''Getting the Basics'' you would be left having to know five terms: *v*isualization, *a*ssociation, *m*emory magic, *c*hunking and *f*ocusing. Because it is hard to get v, a, m, c, f to form a word, you may simply memorize those letters and use them to remind you of the correct words for each.

Memory magic involves quickly finding a ''gimmick'' to help you recreate the important points at a later time. Each listener has to figure out the memory tricks that work for him or her.

Chunking

Chunking involves listening and sorting things into large sections or ''chunks'' for easier recall. The speaker may provide major points or headings. Often the listener has to create order from a large set of information.

Imagine yourself in the following situation. Before leaving for a family vacation your parent gives the following list of things that must be done by Friday.

• stop the mail

• put the dog in a kennel

• buy groceries for the cabin

• get the car checked out

• find the beach balls and inner tubes

• give turtles to Andy

• ask Edna to water the plants and check the apartment

• get new spare tire

As this list is laid out now it would be difficult to remember. How might it be reorganized to make it easier to recall? In other words, what things could you "Chunk" together and remember within the big label? Look at the following two listener reactions.

Listener 1

"I made three chunks:

1. to buy—groceries and tire

2. to care for—dog, turtle, plants

3. to check on—mail, car, play equipment."

Listener 2

"I made three chunks:

1. people—Andy, Edna and Dr. Berkland (the veterinarian at the kennel)

2. shopping—tire and groceries

3. house—mail, beach balls."

Not all information can fit neatly into chunks or packages. Yet creative listeners can find some ways of combining information for easier recall. Read the following list and think about the ways you could "chunk" some of this material.

My Suggestions for Improving Society

1. Reduce the speed limit to 50 mph and save more lives.

2. Require all bus drivers, cab drivers, and department store clerks to take a course in good communication.

3. Require everyone to visit with an older person once a month.

4. Leave the lobbies of city buildings open so people without homes can find a warm place to sleep.

5. Get drunk drivers off the road by taking away their licenses permanently.

6. Provide each adult with a leave of absence from work once during his or her lifetime just for thinking and traveling.

7. Require every high school and college student to work on a soup kitchen line ten times during his or her student career.

8. Create a service semester for students to allow them to work in the community for credit.

You may find some of the following categories helpful as you begin this process: serving the poor, public service, safety, courtesy, personal growth, dignity, communication.

Effective listeners find it very valuable to chunk material in their minds using their thought-speech advantage. Then they can leave the speaker with a firm grasp on the main points.

Focusing

Focusing implies identifying what is most important for you as a listener and working hard to remember that most important part. While listening to a conversation, speech, or class lecture, you will zero in on one or two points and do whatever it takes to remember those points.

Imagine that you heard a speaker describe college scholarship possibilities as follows:

"The following scholarship possibilities might apply to you or to a member of your family. If you wish to apply for a United States Senate Youth Program Scholarship, you must be a high school junior or senior currently serving in a student government elected office and a U.S. citizen. If you wish to apply for a Westinghouse Science Talent Search Scholarship, you must submit a written report on an outstanding independent research project in the area of science, mathematics, or engineering. You must be competing for this scholarship for the first time and must be a high school senior in the United States. If you wish to apply for an Elks National Foundation Scholarship, you must be a high school senior who demonstrates leadership, superior scholarship, and financial need. You must also be a U.S. citizen and reside in the jurisdiction of the Elks.

"There are application forms for these scholarships in the public library reserve room and in the counseling office of the high school."

As you listen, you may focus in on the Westinghouse award because you are a senior and have always been good in science. You may not pay much attention to the other possibilities because you have not been a school leader. So, as you leave the speaker, you may repeat to yourself, "Westinghouse—must describe my research—pick up application at counseling office." Another person may focus by thinking that her daughter has been active in student government and wishes to study government in college. That woman will leave the room focusing in this way, "Senate Youth Program, juniors eligible, elected school officer—library reserve room." Each of you will leave remembering the most important thing for your life.

Listeners may use any of the other thinking techniques to help them focus, but often focusing just involves repeating the important parts to yourself until you are sure you will remember them.

In this section we have looked at specific thinking strategies for getting the basics. These included: (1) visualizaton, (2) association, (3) memory magic, (4) chunking, and (5) focusing. Many listeners use these techniques in combination to make them most effective.

Listening Lab

1. Someone should read aloud the material in → *Listening Practice 18 on pages 105-106* and describe the techniques you would use to remember what you consider important. Compare what you remembered and how you did it with other class members.

2. Have the description of a clothes sale →*Listening Practice 19, page 106* read to you under three different conditions. Discuss how your listening techniques may have changed due to the differing conditions.

Condition 1. A friend mentions a sale that you never heard of before.

Condition 2. You know about the sale, but you can't remember the name and location of the store.

Condition 3. You know about the sale, but you don't know the details of how the prices change over the weekend.

3. Have someone describe the Heimlich Maneuver, a lifesaving technique for aiding a choking victim. →*Listening Practice 20, page 106.* Since this information must be recalled totally, you have to learn all the steps. How will you remember each part of the procedure?

4. You wish to convince your family to let you attend a summer journalism institute, so you need to remember the highlights of the program description. Have someone read →*Listening Practice 21 on page 106* and try to remember what you need to tell your parents about the educational nature of the program.

For further material see →*Listening Practice 22 on page 106,* "Remembering Details."

Following Directions

Each of us spends a great deal of time listening to directions. In a day or a week we may receive many kinds of directions. Think about the past week and check the following areas in which you have listened to directions.

1. _____ meeting someone at a certain place

2. _____ picking someone up from a particular place

3. _____ playing a sport or a musical instrument

4. _____ cooking a certain food or recipe

5. _____ doing specific homework assignments

6. _____ following safety precautions

7. _____ performing efficiently on a job

8. _____ getting from one place to another

9. _____ giving medicine to self or others

10. _____ shopping for food or clothes

11. _____ fixing a machine

12. _____ cleaning a certain place or thing

13. _____ filling out a form

14. _____ creating something artistic

15. _____ caring for another person, animal, or plant

16. _____ relating to another person

Almost everyone would have to check four or five of these situations. Some of you may have checked more than ten. That's because we all listen to directions frequently. Look at the following example:

Put yourself in this situation: You are home alone in the late afternoon when one of your parents calls and gives you directions you must remember to carry out. How will you do it? Listen while someone reads this aloud.

"I need you to do some stuff for me because the boss just called an emergency meeting because of the computer breakdown. I'll be home at least three hours late. Everyone is trying to use this phone so I have to talk fast. Listen carefully. No time to go looking for a pen. Go to Buckley's dry cleaners and get my brown suit before they close at 5:00 P.M. Then call George Matthews and tell him I'll be late for the library board meeting tonight. Take Martha and Todd to the soccer game at 5:30 at the Highpoint Playing Field. Then pick up Fred from his friend Andy's by 5:40. He lives at 2710 Lincolnwood. That's south of Central. Don't use Grant Street to get there. It's all torn up. Then call Luigi's and order a pizza. Get a 16 inch one with no olives or mushrooms. Whatever else you want on it is fine. Feed the kids. If anyone calls, say I'll be home by 8:30. Mrs Turner will bring Martha and Todd home. Bye."

As you followed these directions you probably used many of the techniques we discussed in the earlier sections. For example, repeating some things to yourself, visualizing the route, associating 2710 Lincolnwood with a place where your coach lives—all of these can help you to listen accurately. Yet, listening to directions can be more difficult than other types. It takes some extra techniques. These are: (1) predicting pitfalls, (2) questioning for problem spots, and (3) repeating the highlights.

In the above example, the people, places, and times were critical. You might have recognized a pitfall when you heard "Highpoint Play Field at 5:30" and "Lincolnwood at 5:40." You may realize that it takes at least twenty minutes to make the trip and asked if you could leave Martha and Todd off early or picked up Fred later. In this case the caller indicated one possible problem area by saying, "Don't use Grant Street."

Let's look at the skills of following directions more carefully.

Predicting Pitfalls

It's amazing how a speaker can think things are perfectly clear only to discover how another person can misinterpret the message. A wonderful example of this is contained in a description of teaching by Irving Lee, a famous communication professor. He would ask his classes to tell him how to draw a triangle. Here's what would happen as the directions were called out:

Draw three straight lines connected: he drew them as three sides of a box, or as continuing parts of a single line.

Draw three straight lines touching at their tips: he drew an arrow.

Draw three straight lines connecting them so that they make three angles: he drew them in the form of an X with a line connecting the two lower points. This, of course, made a triangle but with an extra V on top. If they protested that he had now drawn a triangle, he would then ask, "Is this really what you had in mind by a triangle? Have I done exactly what you wanted? Would you be satisfied with an employee who came this close to the assignment? I think not. Try again."

Draw three straight lines connecting them so that they make three and only three angles: he drew a K.

Make three straight lines enclose an area: he drew an A.

Draw three dots: he would put two dots on the blackboard and one on the floor.

Put three dots on the blackboard: he made three dots all on top of each other.

Put three dots on the blackboard not on top of each other: he put one dot on the back of a reversible blackboard, or on the frame of a stationary one.

Put three dots all on the black part of the blackboard: he did as expected.

Now connect the dots: he drew a circle connecting them.

Connect the dots with straight lines: he connected the three dots with only two straight lines, making a V shape.

Connect all three dots with three straight lines: he would take a pencil and draw the third line on the blackboard so that the class couldn't see it.

Now go over the third line with chalk: he used the side of the chalk and smeared it all up.

Put the dots back the way you had them: he did as expected.

Now connect all three dots with three straight chalk lines: he drew dotted lines, or slightly wavy lines, then stood at the side of the blackboard, where he was looking along its surface, and said, "They look straight from here." from *Handling Barriers in Communication* by Irving Lee and Laura L. Lee.

Although most of our misinterpretations are not this dramatic, we can see how unfamiliar language and lack of clarity can lead to confusion.

Unfamiliar Language

Picture yourself in this situation: you are beginning work as a delivery person for a florist. Here's what the boss tells you on your first day.

"Go to the back and pick up a dozen azaleas, fourteen yellow chrysanthemums, eight variegated philodendrom and fifteen gerbera daisies. These all go to the Avanetti family on Walcott Street. To get there, take Tarkenton quite a ways until you see a tall red building with green trim. It will be on your left. Turn there (I think it's Catalpa Avenue) and go about four blocks until you see a stop sign and a house with beautiful peony bushes out front. I think that's Dawson Street. There turn right for one block. The house you want is French Provincial in design and it's on the left near the corner. Leave the flowers under the trellis on the side."

How likely are you to make this delivery correctly and easily? The boss presumes you know types of flowers and home design as well as how to mindread. Words such as "tall," "beautiful," "near," require you to see the world the same way as the speaker does.

Look at the directions below and see how the language itself could sabotage effective listening:

☐ The TV chef says, "Score the flank steak and set aside. Over medium heat in the electric fry pan, saute the onions in four tablespoons butter. Add seasonings and crumbs. Mix well. Take off the heat. Beat egg lightly and add. Spread the mixture over the flank steak and roll up from the long side fastening with skewers. Dredge lightly with seasoned flour. . ."

☐ Your art teacher says, "Draw two isosceles triangles with three-inch sides two inches from each other with their bases parallel. Enclose these triangles in a hexagon. . ."

A careful listener will ask "What does _____ mean?" when following directions depends upon understanding a word or phrase that is unfamiliar. In this way both the sender and the listener make certain that they are using language familiar to both of them.

Clarity

Imagine that in sociology class you have been talking about the roles people play and your teacher assigns the following project. What pitfalls might you foresee for yourself or for others in carrying it out?

"For next week I want you to write a paper describing in detail two or three roles you find yourself in during any given day. Be specific about the image you communicate in each role. For example, you can talk about your language, appearance, attitude, or movements in the following settings—home, school, at work, on vacation, alone, or with a boyfriend or girlfriend. If you don't write very legibly, please type."

What questions might you wish to ask? Most students reported needing a clearer explanation of the following terms: "next week," "paper," "in detail," "image," "legibly." Look at the following examples of trouble spots due to lack of clarity or clear use of terms.

☐ "Oh, I just put in a pinch of salt and sugar."

☐ "It's the loveliest house in town. You can't miss it."

☐ "Don't spend a lot of money on that shirt."

Whereas the language issue raises the question, "What does _____ mean?," the issue of clarity requires another question, namely, "What do you mean by _____ when you use the word?"

Questioning for Problem Spots

Good listeners usually ask speakers to tell them what might be problem spots in the directions. Questions such as "What problems might I run into using these directions?" or "Are there any tricky parts in these directions?" may produce additional needed information. For example, read the following directions and the questions the listener asked.

Speaker: "It's easy to make birdhouses out of milk cartons or food containers. Make small drain holes in the bottom of each house to let rainwater out. Since the top of each house will tilt toward you due to the container shape, put six to eight holes near the front of the bottom. Use an ice pick, or hammer and nail to make the holes. Make the holes from the inside of the container toward the outside whenever you can. When you can't, smooth the edges of the holes with sandpaper. This will let the water drain out better. For a front door make a circle with a pen and cut out the opening with a knife.''

Listener: ''Anything else I should know?''

Speaker: ''Oh yes, small birds such as wrens, sparrows, and bluebirds need small entrances for their houses. Don't make the opening more than 1½ inches.

Listener: ''Where else might I have a problem?''

Speaker: ''Well, be sure to hang it in a shady spot or the heat will kill the eggs.''

Look at the following statements and think about what questions you might ask:

□ ''Leave the paper at my office Friday.''
(Where exactly? Will you be there? Will anyone be there?)

□ ''Then cook the onions.''
(Should they be colorless or should they be brown?)

Now you do the next ones.

□ ''Follow North Avenue until it runs out and you'll be on Belcher Street.''
(—————————————————————)

□ ''Buy five birthday cards while you're at the drug store.''
(—————————————————————)

□ ''Give Jamie the medicine at noon.''
(—————————————————————)

A good listener asks for more information and for problem spots. There is value to the question, ''What else can you tell me about _____?''

Repeating the Highlights

Very often a good listener will repeat back the important parts of a set of directions in order to check out the accuracy of the message. Look at the following example of a set of directions:

''In order to get to Eagle Ridge School you go north on Sherman Avenue for four straight stoplights. Turn left at Applegate and head west for about two miles, past the stables, until you get to a stop sign marked Deerbrook. This is the third or fourth stop sign. Then make a right on Culver. Take that two blocks and the school is on your left side.''

A listener might respond:

''OK. North on Sherman to Applegate, west on Deerbrook. Then right to Culver and it's on the left.''

This response just gives the highlights but it gives the speaker a chance to correct or clarify something that is incorrect or vague. Let's look at another set of directions. How might you summarize this and repeat the highlights for the speaker?

"Cook the onions in the butter until golden. Then add the tomato paste, tomatoes, tarragon, basil, and salt. You probably want to add some water and a teaspoon of sugar. The water will boil off over time. After this has cooked for an hour add the cooked sausage and heat for a half hour. Put in the mushrooms five minutes before you plan to serve the sauce."

When you repeat the highlights, you are giving feedback to the speaker. You give the speaker a chance to add or correct information. See how well this works in the following example of a waiter.

Customer 1: "I'd like a turkey club, hold the mayonnaise, with potato salad on the side. And extra pickle. Plus ice tea."

Customer 2: "I'd like a cheeseburger rare, raw onion, and fries. Ice tea also."

Customer 3: "I'd like a corned beef sandwich on rye with fries, a side order of onion rings, and coffee with cream."

Waiter: "O.K. that's one turkey club, pickle and potato salad. One hamburger with raw onion and fries and one corned beef, fries, and onion rings. Plus two ice teas and a coffee with cream."

Customer 1: "Don't forget, no mayonnaise on the club sandwich."

Customer 2: "That's a cheeseburger, not a hamburger."

If the waiter had not repeated the important points, two customers might have been disappointed.

In this section we have looked at the practical ways for listeners to be sure they are getting accurate and complete directions. Effective listeners will use the following techniques: (1) predicting pitfalls, (2) questioning for problem spots, and (3) repeating the highlights.

Listening Lab

1. Using the diagrams in →*Listening Practice 23, page 107,* have one person verbally describe each diagram and have the rest of the class attempt to reproduce them accurately without seeing them. Share the results and discuss how effective you think the directions were and why.

2. Have someone read the rules for working at a station in a fast-food restaurant →*Listening Practice 24, page 108,* and ask other students to describe how they would remember them and what questions they might ask of the boss who gives these rules.

3. Have each class member develop a set of directions for an "expert" in a certain area and read them to the class. Ask people to identify possible pitfall areas of unfamiliar language and clarity.

4. Read the restaurant orders in →*Listening Practice 25, page 108,* and have individual class members repeat the highlights as if they were waiters or waitresses taking the orders.

5. Read the class assignments which a teacher might give orally → *Listening Practice 26, page 108.* Have class members ask questions to avoid problems and indicate areas of unfamiliar language or poor clarity.

In this chapter we have talked about improving your ability to get basic information. We have looked at increasing your skill by (1) making things memorable, (2) using thinking strategies, (3) finding main ideas, and (4) following directions.

"My assignment is to talk to you for awhile, and yours is to listen to me. I trust we will both finish our work at the same time."

Adlai Stevenson

CHAPTER 4 LISTENING FOR STRUCTURE

Introduction

Whether you are listening to a dinner table argument or to a formal speech, you need to be able to figure out the main points the speakers are trying to make. And if you are listening to a formal speech, you need to recognize how the points relate to each other. To examine how well you do at listening for main points and organization, read the following questions and answer T for true or F for false.

1. _____ I can listen to a friend and realize later that I didn't get the main point of the conversation.

2. _____ I can listen in class and wonder what is important and what is not.

3. _____ I can listen in class and discover that I missed some of the main points.

4. _____ I can listen to a speaker tell a story and not understand how it connects to the rest of the speech.

5. _____ I can listen to speakers and not be able to tell when they are moving from one main idea to another.

6. _____ I can listen to a speech and think that the first ideas do not tie into the other parts of the speech.

7. _____ I can listen to a speech and think that the solution does not really solve the problem the speaker presented.

8. _____ I can listen to another person speak and think, "So what am I supposed to remember?"

9. _____ I can get the point of a speech more easily if the speaker gives me "signposts" or clues that indicate which are the main ideas.

10. _____ I can listen to a speaker and think, "I could have given a much clearer talk in half the time!"

If you answered "true" to three or more questions, this chapter will help you sharpen your knowledge of structure. Effective listeners are able to figure out how verbal information works within a structure. This means they look at the structure of a presentation to tell them what is important and gives them a sense of organizational patterns. Some speakers make this easy because they highlight their main ideas and provide verbal and nonverbal clues to explain the organization. Other speakers tend to give equal emphasis to everything or to ramble. Then, as a listener, you've got your work cut out for you! In order to see how effective listeners look at structures, let's examine the following areas: (1) finding main points, (2) recognizing organizational patterns, (3) finding additional organizational clues.

Finding Main Points

When you find yourself listening to more than pleasant conversation, you need to be able to sort out what is important and what is not. If you can't separate the important ideas from the supporting information, you will never know exactly what the other person is trying to say. Sometimes speakers give you very clear indications of their main points. Other times you have to figure out what is important for yourself.

Someone should read the following teacher's description of how to prepare for an interview. Then see if you can recite the main points when the directions are completed.

Preparing for the Interview

"Before you go out to interview famous persons in our community, you need to go through a series of preparation stages. These people are experts in their fields and they expect you to be prepared to conduct a first-class questioning session. Don't disappoint them! In order to prepare for the interview you can use what I call the STEP system. STEP refers to (1) self, (2) topic, (3) expert, and (4) plan.

Here's how it works.

S ____ Self—Know yourself before you go into the interview situation. Do you have any biases that would cause you to be a poor listener? Have you put aside all other concerns so you can concentrate on the interview?

T ____ Topic—Know something about the subject you are going to talk about. Don't arrive and expect the expert to teach you all the basic stuff. Read or ask questions to help you get a grounding in the area. Know the language!

E ____ Expert—Know something about the person you are interviewing. Be sure you know what he or she does and what you hope to learn. You can find out about experts by reading the books they wrote, listening to their songs, hearing them speak, and by asking them.

P ____ Plan—Plan your questions. Will you ask a number of specific questions, or can you let the subject take as much time as he or she wants with two or three questions? Will you ask open-ended questions that allow the expert to talk about his or her ideas and opinions?

Now that you've learned the STEP system, put it to use. I want to have those local experts call me later and say, "Congratulations, those students were really prepared."

How difficult was it for you to figure out the main points? In this case, the teacher made it easy. She told you that you needed to go through preparation stages, and then she presented them to you twice. She even gave you a memory magic technique, the acronym STEP to help you remember. It should be easy for you to remember *self, topic, expert,* and *plan* as the important points.

Let's look at another example. In this case a teacher is giving directions for evaluating speakers. She talks about how listeners should give feedback to student speakers. There are two rules that she wants the class members to remember. Can you find them? Someone should read this aloud.

Giving Feedback to a Public Speaker

"It's important that you plan ahead when you are giving feedback to a public speaker. You don't just jump in and start rambling because you might overwhelm the speaker with too many details, and you might not stress what you believe are the most important things for the speaker to think about. You need a formula. When you are giving feedback, you need to give the speaker some sense of what worked well—what the person should continue to do again. Therefore, you may wish to start with the things that you liked and be sure you can find something that went well. Then you may wish to move to the problem area or areas. What does this speaker wish to improve before the next speech? So you may mention the areas that did not work very well, and then you may wish to give very specific directions for improving just one or two areas. It's important not to mention fourteen things or the speaker may just give up. So pick out one or two really important things such as eye contact or a strong introduction and talk about them.

"You also want to be careful not to do a great deal of judging, especially at first. So you need to use descriptive language and tell the speaker what you saw or heard. Start there before you go on to say whether you liked what you saw or heard. It's a lot more helpful to hear, "The gestures did not seem to be used to highlight main points," rather than the more general remark, "I didn't like your gestures." If you get into good/bad statements before you describe what actually happened, you may offend the speaker and turn off that person to other useful ideas. So use these two major techniques for giving feedback and you should do well."

If you were a student in this class could you name the two ideas this teacher wanted you to learn about giving feedback to a public speaker? Probably not. →*See Listening Practice 27, page 109, for the answer.*

It is not easy to separate main ideas from supporting ideas, but an effective listener has to learn some techniques. In the next pages we will look at (1) supporting material and (2) main points. Usually the most important ideas are the main ideas. The other material is called supporting material, because it is used to back up the main points. Let's look first at what are not main ideas.

Supporting Material

The purpose of supporting material is to expand upon or to develop the main ideas. Sometimes the speaker makes the main ideas so obvious that you cannot miss them. Often this is not the case. So it may be useful to sort out what are not likely to be the main ideas.

Most of the time the following parts of a verbal presentation are *not* the main ideas but rather serve as supporting material. These are:

1. descriptions—information that helps a listener visualize something

2. humor—jokes, wisecracks, funny stories that may serve to make a point and to gain attention

3. statistics—numerical facts that lend support to a particular point

4. real life examples—stories from actual experience that make a point

5. personal examples—stories from your own life that demonstrate a point

6. stories—narratives or tales that may not be true but that make a point

7. questions—real or rhetorical inquiries that get the listeners to think

8. quotations—statements about the topic by others, usually experts, to give added weight to a point

9. definitions—explanation of what speaker means by a word

Although these elements are important parts of a speaker's material, they seldom contain the actual statements of the main ideas. They may lead up to, or follow, the statement of main ideas.

Look at the following examples of conversation and pick out the various types of supporting material. Note the numbers (1-9, as listed above) next to each selection.

1. _____ "The trees were toppled onto the road. Roots were ripped out of the ground. Thirteen foot waves rose on the lake. Andy and I went down to the breakwater to see the thunderheads roll out of the west. It was the worst storm in many years."

2. _____ "Theologian Morton Kelsey once described listening as. . .being silent with another person in an active way. It is silently bearing with another person. I believe we do not give sufficient value to silence in our relationships. In a world of constant chatter, it is the rare friendship that can sustain quiet moments."

3. _____ "There have been many breakthroughs in science that help us lead healthy lives. One is the discovery of the benefits of fiber in foods. If you base your diet on high fiber foods, you can lose weight and gain other health benefits. Foods high in fiber include beans, bran cereals, cereal products, nuts, and dried fruit. Many vegetables are relatively high in fiber. So eat your corn, carrots, broccoli, and greens. Eat to keep yourself healthy."

4. _____ "How often do you have your eyes checked? I certainly never thought much about it until recently. My last eye examination was eight years ago. I realized that when it got dark that I had trouble seeing the road clearly, but I thought everyone else did, also. I also realized that some people could read signs at a much greater distance than I could, but I thought they were farsighted. Recently when I began to have trouble reading sheet music and seeing the ball during baseball games, I began to think that maybe I had a problem. I finally got around to having an eye examination and discovered that I was seriously nearsighted. I couldn't believe the world when I got my glasses—everything was so big and sharp and clear. So this was what other people were seeing all along! I learned my lesson. Regular eye examinations are an important part of caring for your health!"

5. _____ "How many of you have spent an hour in a car with a four-year-old lately? Raise your hand. Aha! And you survived! But you probably heard things like:"

Kid: Knock, knock.

You: Who's there?

Kid: Apple.

You: Apple who?

Kid: Apple, banana, pear. . .Ha Ha!

"After sixteen of these very strange 'knock-knock' jokes, you are ready to scream. But next time think instead—'This child is practicing language skills.' Maybe that thought will keep you from getting out and walking. What I'm really trying to say is that children need to practice language skills in order to develop their social ability. Therefore, parents, older brothers and sisters, and friends of the family must be subjected to all this practice. Just know that it will pass.''

6. _____ ''According to a study cited in *Megatrends*, soon 75 percent of all jobs will involve working with computers. This means that all high school graduates must be proficient in using, not just familiar with, computers. In a survey of our senior and junior classes only 55 percent of the students had used computers and of this group only 28 percent believed they were proficient. This situation must change before today's freshmen graduate. This school district must provide a computer class for all students.''

Check your responses with the answers in → *Listening Practice 28, page 109.*

As you listen to a speaker you can ask yourself:

1. What point does the speaker seem to be moving toward?

2. How do these examples relate to some main point?

Key Ideas

Now that we have looked at what is *not* the main point, let's turn back to a discussion of what *is* the main point. We can talk about the main point in two ways: as the ''key idea'' when discussing conversational, informal statements and as the ''purpose statement'' when referring to a formal speech. Let's start with the key idea first.

The key idea in a rather short, conversational statement is similar to the topic sentence of a paragraph. The key idea provides a general sense of what the statement is about. It will tell you what to remember. It may come at any point in the overall statement. For example, look at the three versions of the following statement that a person might make, and note the shift in the position of the key idea. Assume there is a conversation taking place about a recent storm.

''<u>It was the worst storm in many years</u>. The trees were toppled onto the road. Roots were ripped out of the ground. Thirteen foot waves rose on the lake. Andy and I went down to the breakwater to see the thunderheads roll out of the west.''

''The trees were toppled onto the road. Roots were ripped out of the ground. Thirteen foot waves rose on the lake. <u>It was the worst storm in many years</u>. Andy and I went down to the breakwater to see the thunderheads roll out of the west.''

''The trees were toppled onto the road. Roots were ripped out of the ground. Thirteen foot waves rose on the lake. Andy and I went down to the breakwater to see the thunderheads roll out of the west. <u>It was the worst storm in many years</u>.''

As a listener, it would not be hard to realize that the speaker's intent is to tell you that it was the worst storm in many years. The rest of the statement provides supporting description. It is likely that the speaker will not expect you to remember the description of the trees or the trip to the breakwater. The point you will be expected to remember is: ''It was the worst storm in many years.''

Now go back to the previous examples 2-6 on pages 54-55 and underline/pick out the key idea in each of them. Check → *Listening Practice 28, page 109,* for the underlining.

As you listen to someone talk, you can ask yourself:

Which sentence provides a general sense of what this statement is about?

What key idea appears to be supported by statistics, quotes, examples, etc?

Purpose Statements

Whereas the key idea refers to the main point of short statements, the purpose statement is found in a speech. The purpose statement in a speech is similar to the thesis statement found in an essay. The purpose statement provides the central idea that controls the shape of the speech. Although some speakers try to create one carefully worded sentence to use as a purpose statement, others may use two or three sentences to form their purpose statement. These statements are found in the introduction to a speech.

The purpose statement should tell the listener about the major points of the speech. For example, if you hear the following statement in the introduction to a speech, what do you think the speech will cover?

"Soccer is a valuable experience because it teaches you athletic skills, keeps you in condition, and gets you involved in extracurricular activities."

You can be almost certain that the speaker will give a three point persuasive speech describing the values of soccer as: (1) teaching athletic skills, (2) keeping you in shape, and (3) involving you in extracurricular activities.

If you hear this sentence in an introduction, what would you predict you will hear during the speech?

"Disney World is a whole recreational park with many distinct units including the Magic Kingdom, Epcot Center, and the River area."

You can be almost certain that the speaker will give a three point informative speech describing Disney World's three major areas.

A more complex purpose statement is found in the introduction to an informative statement by Dwight Conquergood on the flower cloths made by Hmong refugees in the United States. It states:

"This traditional folk art links these women refugees of 1983 with an at least 4000 year old legacy of Hmong mothers teaching their daughters how to embellish everyday life and blend the fanciful with the useful. At the same time this ancient and enduring textile art links Hmong women with other women the world over who have stitched and pieced and sewn their dreams, hopes, and visions into fabrics that are both beautiful and practical."

This introductory statement indicates the listener will hear descriptions of the flower cloths, something about their history, and the visions or dreams these cloths represent. The purpose is to inform the listeners about the cloths and their creators.

Listen to the following introductions to speeches and identify the purpose statements.

Going on a TV Diet

"Recently the A.C. Nielsen Company reported that American teenagers watch about three hours of television a day. Now this is less than the rest of the population watches, but when you think about your sixteen to eighteen waking hours each day, do you really want to spend three of them in front of the tube? If you say 'No,' I have a suggestion for you. Go on a TV diet. It's actually a step-by-step plan to reduce the hours you spend fixed on the screen. Listen carefully as I explain the steps to you."

The Engineering Institute

"Probability and Markov Chains. Digital Logic Design. Robotics. Do any of these words mean anything to you? Can you get excited about them? Do you have five free weeks this summer? If so you should attend the Engineering Institute at Alliance University designed especially for persons interested in careers in engineering. The Engineering Institute is a program taught by nationally known university professors, who introduce future engineers to the many possible areas of study within the field. A summer at Alliance might change your life."

The American Shell

"Americans are people in a shell. We grow up speaking only one language, but the rest of the world is filled with bilingual or trilingual people. When we travel, we expect others to speak to us in English. We do not make any attempts to learn the language or customs of the host country. Americans need education in foreign languages and in the customs of other cultures."

Check your answers with the underlining in → *Listening Practice 29, page 110.*

As you listen to the introductions to speeches, you can ask yourself:

1. Which sentences provide a general sense of what the purpose of this speech will be?

2. How is the purpose statement supported by questions, examples, quotations, statistics etc.?

In this section we have looked at (1) types of supporting material and (2) main points, including key ideas and purpose statements.

Listening Lab

In order to test your ability to recognize main points vs. supporting material, try the following:

1. Assume you are having a conversational discussion with a friend about an important topic. Create a conversational statement of approximately 30 seconds in length that contains a key idea. Have classmates listen to your statement and identify the key idea.

2. One or two people should read the speech *Risk It* by Elissa McBride in → *Listening Practice 30, page 110.* As you listen, try to identify all the types of supporting material she uses. Note a key word next to each type to help you remember the kinds of supports used. In addition, try to identify the main point of her message.

Organizational Patterns

Most formal speeches in lectures have a three-part structure—an introduction, body and conclusion. The structure is similar to that of a composition. The introduction attempts to gain the audience's attention and to tell the listeners about the topic and direction of the speech. The body contains the two, three, or four major points the speaker is making. The conclusion serves to summarize the speaker's message and to end the speech in an interesting and memorable way. In this section, we will focus on the body of the speech, which contains the structure or organizational pattern.

There are a number of common organizational patterns that listeners need to be able to recognize. These include:

1. chronological order

2. spatial order

3. topical order

4. process order

5. problem-solution order

6. inductive order

7. motivated sequence order

Let's look at each of these to help you recognize them.

Chronological Order

Chronological order refers to placing the points of the speech into a time pattern. The speaker may talk about time in terms of the past, present, and future. Time may refer to predicting the future or placing historical events in sequence. Or time may refer to smaller segments such as morning, noon, and night. You will recognize the chronological pattern because it follows a time-oriented order. This time-oriented pattern is easy to follow because you are able to see the logical movement through a chronological order. Some topics that might be time oriented include:

• the history of air travel

• the past and future of the Olympics

• plans for building the community center

Some sample purpose statements that tell you the speaker will use a chronological pattern are:

□ ''For the next few minutes I would like to describe the seven days of the Outward Bound program that you will attend.''

□ ''Let me review how we got to this point in genetic research and tell you about the future of this research as I see it developing in the next 20 years.''

Spatial Order

Spatial order refers to organizing information based on the physical relationship of people, places, or objects. You may realize that a speaker is talking about experiences or people in one place and then moving on to another place. Some topics that might be spatially organized would include:

• historical sites in New England

• the neighborhoods of San Francisco

• our vacation walking the Appalachian Trail

• the religions of China and India

Some sample purpose statements that tell you the speaker will use a spatial pattern are:

□ ''As an exchange student I had the opportunity to live for three months in three different cities, Munich, Hamburg, and Berlin. Let me tell you a little bit about each of them.''

□ ''The movement of the Mormon faith may be traced from the East coast to the Midwest and finally to its Western center. Each place represents a significant phase in the development of the faith.''

This place-oriented pattern may be fairly clear, but if the speaker does not indicate clearly the shifts from place to place, you may become confused.

Topical Order

Topical order refers to dividing a whole topic into natural parts. There is no necessary sequence. Any point could be first or last. Yet together these points will tell the listener a great deal about the overall topic. Some ideas that might be organized by topic are:

• famous newscasters

• types of video games

• the paintings of Andrew Wyeth

• understanding the library

Some sample purpose statements that tell you a speaker will use a topical order are:

□ ''To fully appreciate your visit to historical Williamsburg, you need to experience the historical buildings, the craft demonstrations, the ceremonies and the restaurants.''

□ ''The success of this art center rests with three factors: faculty, facilities, and funding. We need to look at each of these in depth.''

This topical order pattern will work well if speakers note the topics to be covered and then indicate clearly when they are moving from one point to another.

Process Order

Process order refers to explaining the way something works. The speaker explains the steps in a process from beginning to end. By nature, a process involves a logical order that must be understood by the listener in order to use the information. Some topics that might be organized in terms of process include:

• screening your own T-shirts

• the making of music videos

• creating homemade pizza

Some sample purpose statements that tell you the speaker will use a process pattern are:

□ ''There are five steps to taking great pictures with this camera.''

□ ''If you want to become a naturalized citizen, you must go through a very specific set of procedures. It will save you a lot of time to do this paperwork in the right order.''

The process order should be extremely clear. The listener should understand exactly which step follows the last one. It is important for the listener to be able to review each step, in order.

Problem-Solution Order

Problem-solution order refers to organizing information around two major areas—the (1) problem or problems and (2) the solution or solutions. Listeners are likely to hear the description of some serious problem, and then they will hear one or more solutions that might solve or reduce the problem. Some topics that might be organized in terms of problem-solution order include:

- the rising national debt

- the lack of adequate day-care facilities

- acid rain and pollution

- the rising cost of college tuition

Some sample purpose statements that tell you a speaker will use a problem-solution pattern are:

☐ ''The unemployment problems of our cities are choking this nation. We must find relief from this crisis. In my following remarks, I wish to detail the extent of the problem and propose alternative suggestions for alleviating this major national problem.''

☐ ''In order to reverse the pollution from acid rain, we need to understand the extent of the damage and to mount a three-pronged attack to prevent more extensive pollution.''

The problem-solution order usually occurs when the speaker is trying to persuade the listener to believe something or to do something. The listener needs to understand the problem fully and to grasp the connections between the problem described and the solutions that are proposed. Throughout the speech, the listener is paying attention to the information and to how he or she feels about the problem and the solution.

Inductive Order

Inductive order refers to organizing facts or examples to build to a conclusion. The listeners may be unaware of the speaker's exact point until near the end of the speech. Almost any persuasive topic could be developed in an inductive order, so long as the speaker does not mind holding back the actual point of the speech until late in the presentation. This delayed statement of the main point may keep some listeners actively involved; others may get turned off or frustrated. Usually the speaker hopes the listeners will reach the same conclusion as the speaker by hearing all the evidence. Some sample topics that might be inductively organized include:

- reforming the juvenile courts

- adopting handicapped children

- funding for gifted programs in the schools

- donating to local charities

- raising salaries for educators

Some sample purpose statements that tell you the speaker will use an inductive order are:

☐ "Let me tell you how handicapped people move about in our city now and I'll let you draw your own conclusions about this way of life."

☐ "I would like you to picture a number of prison situations with me and then decide what might or should be done about them."

This inductive pattern can present problems for a listener. You may find yourself becoming frustrated or confused if you are not certain what the speaker is trying to do. If the speech is well handled, you may be fascinated and curious to reach the conclusions and to see the pieces pulled together. The listener must work during this speech because it is vital to follow each piece and work to put them together.

Motivated-Sequence Order

Motivated-sequence order refers to a specific pattern for persuasive speeches developed by the late Alan Monroe, professor at Purdue University. There are five steps to this pattern: (1) attention, (2) need, (3) satisfaction, (4) visualization and (5) action. The speaker tries to get the listeners' attention and to describe some problem or situation that needs to be changed. Then the speaker proposes one or more solutions to solve or satisfy the problem. In the visualization step, the speaker tries to describe or picture the benefits of these solutions for the listeners, and finally the speaker details actions the listeners could take to relieve the problem. Some topics that might be organized in terms of motivated sequence order include:

• teenage unemployment

• cost of medical care

• illegal immigration

• athletic payoffs

Some sample purpose statements that tell you the speaker will use a motivated-sequence pattern are:

☐ "Now that we've laughed at the joke, let me turn to the serious side of the issue—the loss of our forests and what we can do about it. I'll paint a picture of the real and ideal future and you can decide which you want to live in, and what you are willing to do about it."

☐ "I'll give some shocking statistics about child abuse, describe the problem in our city, point out new directions, describe the benefits of these directions and ask for your support in my fight for children's lives."

The motivated-sequence order always involves a persuasive situation. The listener will be asked to take some action, so you have to pay careful attention in order to understand the problem, the solutions, and what will be expected of you. Then you can decide what action, if any, you wish to take.

In this section we have looked at some common organizational patterns. The possible structures you will hear are (1) chronological order, (2) spatial order, (3) topical order, (4) process order, (5) problem-solution order, (6) inductive order, and (7) motivated sequence order. The last three are most likely to be found when you are hearing a persuasive speech. Listen carefully for that structure and you will be able to remember the speech far more easily.

Listening Lab

In order to test your ability to recognize organizational patterns, try the following:

1. Have each person create and deliver an introduction to a speech containing (a) an attention-getting device and (b) a purpose sentence. After hearing the introduction, tell the speaker what points you expect to hear during the speech.

2. Ask people to read the brief speeches in → *Listening Practice 31, page 111.* As listeners, identify the structure used and describe the main points in the body of each speech.

3. Look at each of the following topics, and suggest one or two organizational patterns that you are most likely to hear if you listen to a speech on that subject. You may also indicate one or two organizational patterns that a speaker would be *unlikely* to use for that topic.

   1. the life cycle of the hummingbird

   2. traveling through the Yukon

   3. the cost of being buried

   4. the dangers of smoking

   5. financing a college education

   6. preparing for an interview

   7. families of the future

   8. U.S. Colonial history

   9. motherhood

  10. the best of the rock videos

  11. finding help for alcoholism

  12. using your videotape camera effectively

More Organizational Clues

As you listen to speakers, you generally pick up quickly the ways they move from one point to another and how they stress their main points. As a listener, you can look for the verbal and nonverbal clues that signal a transition, you can listen for repetition or predictions that remind you of the structure, and you can ask questions to clarify any confusion about structure. Let's look at each of these clues separately.

Transitions

One way to tell if a speaker is moving from one point to another is to look for transition words or phrases. Transitions are those words or phrases that form bridges or links between one idea and another. After a speaker has made a point, he or she usually indicates to the listeners that a new idea is coming right along and that it is connected to the earlier idea. In the following example, a speaker concludes a point on the recent growth of radio and moves into discussing cable television.

□ ''. . .radio has found a place in the sun again. In addition, we are witnessing the tremendous growth of cable television which. . .''

In this case the phrase "in addition" indicates a shift linking the previous idea (radio) to the new discussion of television. Read the following statements and identify the ideas being linked through the transition statement.

□ "In addition to finding volunteers from a young population, you can also turn to retired persons who are seeking something valuable to do with their time."

□ "Now that we have examined some of the language of the stock market, let's turn to the process of finding a stock broker.

□ "In contrast to the mountains of New Mexico, the Colorado Rockies show their flowers. . ."

When linking large discussions of ideas, the transitions phrases usually include the last point and the future point. When linking ideas in quick succession, you may find the speaker uses a series of transition words instead. These are easily recognized. For example, read the following set of directions for safety on an aircraft and pick out or underline the words that serve as transitions between ideas.

"Let me review our air/regulations for you. All carry-on luggage must be stored under the seat. Hanging clothes may be placed on hangers at the front of the aircraft. Overhead racks are for light items such as coats and hats. We do this so heavy things will not fall on passengers during turbulence. As an additional safety factor, we ask that your seat belt remain fastened at all times unless you need to use the rest rooms. Your seat belt must be fastened during takeoff and landing and when the seatbelt light is on. Also we ask that you do not operate a radio during flight as it might interfere with navigation equipment and it might disturb other passengers. In keeping with our concern for passenger enjoyment, we ask that you smoke only in the smoking sections. You may not smoke cigars or pipes. Smoking is prohibited during takeoff and landing. Finally, we ask that you remain in your seats until the plane has reached the gate and come to a complete stop. These regulations should make your flight safe and comfortable."

→ See Listening Practice 32, page 112, for answers.

The following words are sample transition words or phrases that may serve as verbal clues that the speaker is moving from one point to another.

meanwhile	moving to	at the same time
first, second	but	thus
also	again	in contrast
next	on the contrary	in conclusion
another	in other words	because
as a result	to sum up	since
finally	another point	similarly
in addition to	moreover	yet
in the same way	nevertheless	inasmuch as
for example	on the other hand	in the second place

for instance	otherwise	although
furthermore	then	instead of
however	therefore	even though

Speakers usually accompany these transition words with nonverbal clues. Many speakers will take a step or two when switching from an old point to a new one. Others will use hand gestures to indicate a shift in topic. You may see a speaker use fingers to indicate first, second, or third. The phrase "on the other hand" may be accompanied by an appropriate hand movement. Frequently speakers will pause or use silence to indicate the end of one point and the beginning of another. This silence adds to your thought-speed time and allows you to put things together in your mind before hearing new words.

Repetition

There is an old adage that instructs speakers how to keep listeners on track. "Tell them what you're going to tell them. Tell them. Then tell them what you told them." Although this may sound excessive, very few listeners would get lost if a speaker used these directions. As a listener, you have to pay close attention for the speaker's repetition, which tells you the main ideas and order of the speech.

When speakers give long addresses, they usually indicate the main points in the introduction and review them in the conclusion. For example, the speech on the sections of Disney World might have the following sentences in the introduction (I) and conclusion (C).

☐ (I) "...Disney World is a whole recreational park. I will talk about the areas I find most exciting, the Magic Kingdom, Epcot Center, and the River area."

☐ (C) "...So the next time you get to Florida, do spend a few days at Disney World and be sure to see my favorite places, the Magic Kingdom, Epcot Center, and the River area."

Sometimes the repetition is found only in the conclusion. A speaker may wind up the introduction of a speech on the family by saying, "In the next few minutes I'll share some of the recent thinking about families with you." Then in the conclusion you may hear, "Remember, (1) There is no right way to be a family, (2) the family must be viewed as a system and (3) developing strong relationships in families takes time and work."

Sometimes the best way to repeat a point is to make it visual. When speakers use a chart or chalkboard, they are repeating the idea in a visual way. If you have heard it and seen it, you are far more likely to remember the point than if you have just heard it or just seen it.

Predictions

How many times have you sat through a class lecture and wondered what you needed to remember? How many times did you fill a notebook with words but fail to sort out what was critical? This might have been avoided if the speaker had told you what to listen for.

One way a speaker can help the listener is to indicate directly and exactly what should be remembered. A speaker may say, "I'll be talking a great deal about the settlement of the Northwest, but what I want you to remember are the four main explorers and the routes they took." Or, "I'll be describing Vincent Van Gogh's childhood, and I want you to listen for those things that might have influenced his painting." By predicting the important points, the speaker allows the listener to sort out what is important from what is unimportant.

Questions

What happens if the speaker does not have a clear purpose sentence and does not summarize the points in the conclusion? What happens if the transitions are not very clear? What's a listener to do? As we said before, listening is *doing*. And this is the time for the listener to work out loud.

As a listener, you need to ask questions if you are lost or confused. During some speeches or class lectures, you may be encouraged to interrupt with questions. At other times, you must wait until the presentation is completed to ask. If you are sitting close to a speaker, your nonverbal feedback—such as a puzzled look—may serve as a kind of question. Questions such as the following allow the listener to get information about main points or organizational patterns.

1. "Would you please explain that last point again?"

2. "You said there were five steps, and I only picked out four. Would you review the steps again?"

If you have heard the speaker before and you know you may get lost in details, you may ask structural questions before the speech, such as "What should we listen for during your presentation?" or "What types of information do you want us to remember?" This helps the speaker clarify goals, and he or she may even repeat the main points during the speech.

Most speakers are flattered by questions because they indicate the listeners are interested. Questions serve to provide you with important information. Don't hesitate to ask them.

Listening Lab

1. Have someone read the selections in → *Listening Practice 33, page 113,* and identify the transitions.

2. Of twelve volunteers, six are to leave the room. Read material in → *Listening Practice 34, page 113,* to the remaining group giving no prediction clues. Then ask the test questions that follow the selections. Then call in the second group of volunteers and read the same material, giving prediction clues. Compare their responses to the questions.

3. Have someone read the selections in → *Listening Practice 35, page 114,* and list questions you might wish to ask the speaker.

In this chapter, we have described how effective listeners figure out the structure of a short or long presentation. We examined the following actions a listener could take: (1) finding main points, (2) recognizing organizational patterns, and (3) finding additional organizational clues. We hope you will try to use these approaches in your everyday listening behavior.

"The spoken word belongs half to those who speak, and half to those who hear."
French proverb

CHAPTER  ANALYZING PERSUASION

Introduction

Every day you are bombarded with a variety of persuasive messages. Sales people tell you about their products; cashiers in fast-food restaurants make a "suggestive sell" of just one more item; friends convince you to go places and do things; the boss tries to get some extra work from you; a teacher tries to convince you of the importance of a particular subject. You can get exhausted just thinking about it! Some of us get so overwhelmed with the thought of dealing with all these messages that we let them wash over us and make very few thoughtful responses. To think about how you analyze the persuasive messages around you, read the following statements and mark each one T for true or F for false.

1. _____ I tend to buy products because I have heard the names before.

2. _____ I find political speeches and debates too hard to follow, so I usually don't listen very carefully.

3. _____ I hate to say no to my friends, so I usually do what they want.

4. _____ I tend to give in when someone plays on my emotions.

5. _____ I should ask for more information from speakers but I feel uncomfortable doing so and I keep my mouth shut.

6. _____ I am often swayed in my thinking by a person who appears confident and self-assured.

7. _____ I will often go along with other people to keep them from being angry or upset with me.

8. _____ I know people are using persuasive strategies on me, but I just can't name them or describe them.

9. _____ I have a hard time dealing with telephone salespeople, so I stay on the line even if I don't want to buy anything.

10. _____ I can get overwhelmed in an argument when someone throws facts and statistics at me.

Most people answer "T" true to many of these statements. If you find yourself in this group, it's time to consider the hard work of listening to persuasive messages—and to respond to these messages.

Effective listeners understand the process of persuasion, can sort out a persuader's techniques, and decide how to respond to a persuasive message. To see how effective listeners examine persuasive messages, let's look at the following areas: (1) understanding the persuasive process, (2) developing critical listening skills, (3) analyzing a persuader's appeals, and (4) recognizing propaganda devices.

The Persuasive Process

Persuasion is an important part of your everyday life. This process can affect you in many positive and negative ways. And you can be sure of one thing—it will affect you. In order to understand the persuasive process, let us examine two areas: a definition of persuasion and your persuasibility.

Persuasion Defined

We can describe persuasion as a communication process designed to change your beliefs or to move you to action. A persuader (formal speaker, advertiser, friend) chooses a message to influence your beliefs about a certain subject and/or to influence your actions related to that subject. The verbal and nonverbal parts of this message are carefully adopted to *you*— either to you as an individual or to you as a member of a particular group.

There are two general types of persuaders: the coactive persuaders and the coercive persuaders. The coactive type of persuader tries to show how your ideas are related to his or her ideas and how you will benefit from a specific belief or action. The coercive persuader will try to force you into a belief or action, often with threats. With a coercive persuader, you have the feeling that you are moving against your own will. Read each of the following persuasive messages aimed at getting older citizens to support a school bond referendum. Identify one as coercive and one as coactive.

"You have been an active member of this community and always supported the schools when your own children were younger. Now we need to pass the school board referendum to see that your grandchildren and their friends have the same wonderful educational opportunities as your children did. Please vote 'yes' with us on Tuesday."

"There's a school bond referendum coming up and we need your vote. If the referendum does not pass, these schools will continue to go downhill and this will affect our real estate values. You could lose all the money you've put into your house. You had better vote 'yes' on Tuesday."

As a listener, you pick up the tone of the message, which tells you whether the persuader is working with you and your ideas or beliefs, or whether you are being threatened. Although both types of persuaders may get their desired results, one leaves listeners feeling good about themselves and the other leaves listeners angry or intimidated. Yet no matter how talented persuaders are, their effectiveness is tied to your ability to be persuaded. Let's examine just that point.

Your Persuasibility

We believe there are two main factors that affect your persuasibility— your needs and your connection to a particular topic. Let's look at each of these separately.

Your Needs as a Listener

Psychologist Abraham Maslow identified a hierarchy or scale of human needs that are common to all human beings. He arranges human needs on a scale from very basic needs to higher order needs and suggests that persuaders should adapt their messages to the needs of particular listeners. To understand this more clearly, look at Maslow's list of human needs ranging from the most basic to those of a higher order.

1. Physiological needs—We need such basic things as food, drink, and shelter.

2. Safety and security needs—We need protection from threats and danger. We prefer to stick to familiar things and we like to know what is going to happen. We need to feel safe now and in the future.

3. Belonging and love needs—We need warmth and affection, and a sense of being part of a group. We value connectedness to others.

4. Esteem needs—We need to feel that we have independence and freedom; competence or strength in certain areas; respect, recognition, and appreciation. We need a sense of status and importance.

5. Self-actualization needs—We need to do what fulfills us and makes us feel good about ourselves. We need to fulfill our potential *for our own sake.*

Let us look at how a persuader might adapt to the needs of different listeners using an example from a business setting. Recently a large corporation moved from a location downtown in the city to a suburban location and tried to persuade the employees to remain with the corporation. Upper-level managers met with small groups of employees to try to persuade them to stay with the organization.

Although some of the same arguments were used at all meetings, the managers adapted their messages to the type of group they were addressing. For example, when talking with a group of lower paid clerical workers, the management teams talked in terms of security needs. They suggested that it would be difficult to find a new job in the current economic climate. They promised extra money to those who worked in the new location and they promised transportation help—money to pay for extra carfare or special buses. They also explained how the new building would be safer than the old rickety one the firm was leaving.

As these managers talked with the professional employees who already made very good salaries, they used other strategies. They appealed to the esteem and status needs of these employees, promising them fancier offices and better working conditions. They also described a bright future of moving up the corporate ladder in an organization that would expand in the new location. Although the basic point was the same—''We want you to keep your job and work in our new location''—the specific messages were adapted to the listeners' needs.

The following arguments might be used to persuade people to move from an old corporate building to a new one a distance away. Which needs do each of these messages appeal to most strongly? Refer to the needs list developed by Maslow, items 1 through 5. Some may contain more than one.

1. _____ You've been with this company for twelve years and are part of the team. It would be hard for you to start over with new people, and you would be sorely missed by the rest of us here.

2. _____ There will be guards in the parking lot at all times. If you have to work overtime, there will be a shuttle bus leaving every hour to take people into the city. Or the company will pay for you to take a cab.

3. _____ At this location, we will have the space to develop a full athletic facility. There will be a pool and gymnasium with weight lifting equipment and basketball facilities. There will be a jogging path around the building. Your family members are also welcome to use these facilities.

4. _____ If you look at the map of this area, you will notice that eight of the big corporations for our region have already moved their headquarters to this location. We are just following the lead of other major organizations. By now, there are fine restaurants and entertainment facilities in the area.

5. _____ If you are going to feed your family, you need this job. This is not the time to be pounding the pavements looking for a new one.

6. _____ This facility will encourage you to work to the best of your capacity. You can work on a flexible schedule, and you will have the space to house the support staff you have always wanted.

7. _____ In our estimation about seventy-five percent of the employees will move with us, so you will continue to have the same people around you. Your friends' faces will still greet you each day in our new location.

Effective listeners paid careful attention to these messages because they knew the company was trying to persuade them to move. In some cases, the employees were delighted at the opportunity and did not need to be persuaded. In other cases, it was difficult to find the right way to convince people to make such a big move. The success of the persuaders hinged on their ability to find the right way to appeal to each person's needs. As a listener, if you do not see how your needs will be met, you will reject a message.

Your Connection to a Topic

In addition to your general needs, your particular position on a topic affects your persuasibility. There are four factors that determine your particular connection to a topic:

(1) The action is not connected in a negative way to a large number of important areas of your life.

(2) The idea or action has not been publicly opposed by you or people who are very close to you.

(3) The idea or action does not threaten your self-image.

(4) You are not a closed-minded person.

Let's look briefly at each of these factors:

(1) The action is not connected in a negative way to a large number of important areas of your life. It would be difficult to persuade you to believe something or do something if such a belief or action would affect important areas of your life negatively. For example, if you were devoted to your family and wanted to spend as much time as possible with your family, you might resist the managers' persuasive messages to take a job at a faraway location. Working at the new location might mean long hours commuting and would take you away from the family many more hours per week. In addition, if you were a strong community supporter and you believed this move would take many jobs out of your community, you might resist even harder the appeal to move. It is very difficult to persuade a listener who sees that the suggested idea or action would negatively affect important areas of his or her life.

(2) The idea or action has not been publicly opposed by you or by people who are close to you. If you have been an outspoken opponent of an idea, you will be very hard to persuade. For example, if you had led an employee organization opposed to the move before it became final, it would be difficult to persuade you to follow the company to a distant suburb. If your boss or co-workers whom you respected had opposed the move actively, it would also be difficult to persuade you. If you had not taken a public stand and your closest co-workers had not either, you would be easier to persuade. You would not lose face or look as if you were backing down. Usually the person who makes public statements believes strongly in an idea and has developed arguments for his or her position. This is a hard listener to reach.

(3) The action does not threaten your self-image. The way you see yourself is directly tied to your persuasibility. If you think you will lose face by going along with an idea or action, such as moving to a new location in order to continue working for the company, you will be very difficult to persuade.

But if you do not see your self-image threatened by a particular action, then you will be more persuasible. We tend to be very careful of our self-images because we have to live with ourselves. If a persuader tries to get you to do something that will conflict with your own self-image, you are likely to resist.

(4) You are not a closed-minded person. Some people see the world in black and white terms, while others see it in shades of gray. If you see things in black and white, it means you are likely to view things as good or bad, right or wrong, and you are not likely to change. Your mind is closed to other possibilities. It is very difficult to persuade a closed-minded person to believe or do something that he or she does not already agree with because that person will tune out the speaker. For example, a closed-minded employee would tell the management team, ''This is a stupid idea. I opposed it from the first and nothing you say will change my mind.'' An open-minded person is one who can see advantages and disadvantages to opposing positions. This person is flexible and willing to listen to arguments. Such a person would say, ''I've not been in favor of this move, but I'm willing to listen to your arguments in favor of moving.'' If you are an open-minded person, you are more persuasible than if you are closed-minded.

Listening Lab

In order to become more familiar with some of these concepts, try the following:

1. Have someone read the messages in → *Listening Practice 36, page 114,* and identify them as coming from coercive or coactive persuaders.

2. Listen to the specific arguments in → *Listening Practice 37, page 115,* and identify the needs to which the speaker is appealing.

Critical Listening Skills

Alert listeners must be prepared to listen critically when responding to persuasive messages. The persuader may exaggerate, omit information, or manipulate the facts in order to make a point. As a listener, you have to sort through all the information and make judgements about which information and arguments are valid and which are misleading. To develop your detection abilities to full capacity, you need four critical listening skills: (1) recognizing loaded language, (2) distinguishing between fact and opinion (3), identifying inferences, and (4) evaluating sources.

Recognizing Loaded Language

Loaded language carries strong emotional meaning. It calls forth an emotional response of a positive or negative nature. Such language may move you to tears, anger, or great excitement. For example, in the United States today people sometimes say that if you wish to appeal to the patriotism of an audience, you should talk about ''Mom, the flag, and apple pie.'' These are examples of symbols and terms that most people would consider loaded with meaning. The terms ''communism,'' ''nuclear war,'' ''rock music,'' ''adoptee's rights,'' ''birth control,'' ''racism,'' and ''divorce'' represent words that many people find loaded.

Sometimes you don't realize something is loaded, until you understand how else a statement might be worded. Look at the following paired statements. Identify the statement that contains loaded words.

1a. He was seen lurking behind the victim's house

1b. He was seen standing behind Mrs. Marzaro's house

2a. "Old Iron Claws" ripped out the stitches, and the wound began to hemorrhage.

2b. The doctor took out the stitches and wound began to bleed.

3a. He gunned his sports car and rear-ended a brand new station wagon.

3b. He pulled out and hit the bumper of the green station wagon.

As you probably guessed, the first sentence in each pair contains the loaded language. For example, it is very different to form an image of someone as "lurking" rather than the more neutral "standing." Calling Mrs. Marzaro a "victim" is an emotional way of indicating how the speaker views the situation.

Because words have various connotations—implied meanings or associations—the same term appears in an unfavorable light to one listener and a favorable light to another one. A third listener may have a neutral reaction to the same term. Look at the following words and categorize them as favorable, neutral, or unfavorable according to your personal experience

· Native American, Indian, Redskin

· commune, group, mob, community, crowd

· young, green, beginner, naive

· minuscule, tiny, small, petite, little, short

· child, brat, youngster, kid, toddler, baby

· jalopy, car, wheels, vehicle

As people try to persuade each other, they sometimes label each other with loaded terms when the same point could be made with purely descriptive terms. Read the following paired sentences and decide which you would rather hear as a listener:

1a—You are inconsiderate.

1b—You interrupt me when I am making my points.

2a—You are selfish.

2b—You plan the vacations you enjoy, but we never go to the places I want to visit.

3a—You are self-centered.

3b—You always forget my birthdays.

 As a listener, you need to identify the points at which a speaker starts to play on your emotions by using loaded language. Then you can try to sort out the point of the message from the emotional overtones.

Distinguishing between Fact and Opinion

Frequently it is difficult to recognize the difference between what is a fact and what is a speaker's opinion. Some persuaders are careless and present their opinions as fact; others try to mislead listeners by confusing fact and opinion. Only an alert listener can recognize the problem. The word ''fact'' means an event or truth that is known to exist or has been observed. It is information that can be checked out as either correct or incorrect. On the other hand, ''opinion'' reflects a speaker's attitudes or feelings.

Read the following paired sentences and try to identify the one containing the fact and the one containing the opinion:

1a. Mark is a gifted pianist and prodigy.

1b. Mark can play Brahms, and he is six years old.

2a. Movies are too violent these days.

2b. The last four movies I saw had bloody scenes in them.

3a. Rosecrest College is for the ''brains.''

3b. Rosecrest College only admits students in the top ten percent of their graduating class.

You probably figured out that the first sentence of each pair contained the opinion of the speaker, while the second sentence contained information. Usually facts serve as the basis of a person's opinions, but listeners need to know the facts to evaluate the speaker's opinion.

The following statements are quotations from people a camp director called trying to get recommendations for prospective camp counselors.

□ ''Juan is an intelligent, personable, and dedicated young man. He will be a fine camp counselor.''

□ ''Charmain is an outgoing, talented, and perceptive person. I think you will be lucky to have her on your staff.''

□ ''Francine has a wonderful way with children. You really should hire her.''

If you were the camp director, what questions would you ask these people? If you were one of the people being asked for a recommendation, what types of information could you provide which might provide factual support for your opinion of this applicant? For example, if asked, the second speaker may explain Charmain is ''outgoing'' because she has led a Scout troop for three years and calls the children in the troop at home to be sure they know what is going on. She is ''talented'' because she involves the children in creative drama and because she has acted in four community productions. Finally, she is ''perceptive'' because she has called parents to discuss whether something is wrong when a child appears worried or sad. This type of specific descriptive information based on fact would be far more helpful to the camp director than the labels that reflect the speaker's opinion. An alert listener who hears opinions ask the questions ''what facts are provided to justify the opinion? Is the opinion justified by the facts?''

Identifying Inferences

In addition to distinguishing between fact and opinion, a listener needs to be able to identify inferences made by a speaker. Inferences are assumptions, guesses, or predictions about the future based upon the factual evidence at hand and the speaker's competence to make informed judgments. Look at the following sets of related sentences and pick out the factual statement, the opinion statement, and the inference:

1a. Mom has just seen the sixteen broken glasses in the kitchen.

1b. Mom is mad.

1c. Mom is going to ground us for a month.

2a. It is four in the afternoon and the sky has become almost black.

2b. This is awful weather.

2c. We are in for a tornado.

In each of the sets of sentences, the first statement is fact and the second is opinion. The third sentence represents inferences drawn from previous facts and opinion. The inferences might be correct. Yet, Mom might be forgiving. A tornado might not come. Inferences are predictions, not facts.

Read the following development of inferences in more complicated situations:

□ In history class a teacher may encounter a student named Lee who uses a range of resources and arguments in writing term papers and who speaks frequently in class discussions. The teacher may reach the opinion, "Lee is a good researcher and speaker." The teacher may then make the inference, "Lee would be a valuable addition to the debate team." Lee might become an excellent debater, or Lee might become very anxious making formal arguments against opponents.

□ If you are a runner who competes in track meets, you may look at some opponents' records and reach the opinion, "they aren't very good on the hurdles," and then infer, "I can beat them all." You might beat them all or someone might get that extra "kick" and beat you.

Inferences seem so natural and obvious that sometimes listeners do not realize that they are not facts. Remember that they are predictions, or guesses. Different speakers may reach different inferences from the same factual data. Therefore, you must separate facts, opinions, and inferences.

Evaluating Sources

Suppose you were at a party and heard a stranger say, "In a nuclear attack, it is absurd to suppose that a survival shelter and a few feet of dirt will protect a living organism within a mile of ground zero." What would you like to know about that person? In our world of constant communication, we are bombarded with countless pieces of contradictory information and countless opinions and inferences based on this information. How do we know what to believe? One important piece of advice for making sense of persuasive messages remains "consider the source." Ask yourself, "What makes a source believable for me on a particular topic?" Given the following topics, what credentials would you wish a speakers to have to address you on each of these?

• the value of a vegetarian diet

• teaching your child to read

• preparing for an employment interview

• the role of cable television in the history of media

• famous coaches of the National Football League

Although your expectations would differ according to each topic, you should have some basic criteria for judging the speaker's familarity with the topic. Consider these questions as the basis for your criteria:

1. Is the speaker an authority on this topic? What is the speaker's experience with the topic?

2. Is the speaker unprejudiced? If not, what prejudices does the speaker hold?

3. Is the speaker trustworthy and reliable?

4. Why did the speaker choose this topic?

Very often famous people complain that because they are known in one area, such as entertainment or sports, people wish to hear their opinions on everything from child rearing to economic policy. Unfortunately some popular media figures have given their names and support to causes with which they were only slightly familiar. Just as you would not want a famous labor leader performing your appendectomy, neither would you want a famous physician speaking to you on labor unions unless this was an additional area of the doctor's expertise. Listeners must always ask, "Is the source an authority on *this topic?* What is the source's experience with topic?"

Sometimes persuaders claim to be unbiased, but you can tell quickly that they feel rather strongly about a particular idea or action. On the other hand, some speakers explain their bias or prejudices clearly to the audience and then go ahead and examine the topic. In such a case, the audience can then analyze the information with an understanding of the speaker's perspective. A teacher may say, "I happen to believe in this position. You don't have to accept it, but you need to know where I stand and why I may stress certain ideas." A listener who knows nothing about a speaker's biases is at a disadvantage.

It is important to know if a source can be trusted. The speaker's reputation, appearance, or general manner may make you distrust the message you are receiving. It is critical that you can trust a source. If not, the whole message becomes unbelievable.

Finally you may wish to know why the person is taking a particular position. Is the person truly concerned about the topic? Is the person trying to impress you or someone else? Does the speaker expect anything from you in response? Listeners need to think, "What are the speaker's motives for talking on this topic in this way?"

In this section, we have examined the critical listening skills of (1) recognizing loaded language, (2) distinguishing between fact and opinion, (3) identifying inferences, and (4) evaluating sources.

Listening Lab

1. Have someone read the material in →*Listening Practice 38, page 115,* and identify the examples of loaded language in the paragraphs.

2. Number your paper 1 to 21. Listen to someone read the 21 sentences from →*Listening Practice 39, page 115,* and note F for fact, I for inference, and O for opinion next to each number.

3. Have someone read the statements in →*Listening Practice 40, page 116,* and either indicate that you think the source is valid, or list the questions you would ask about the source in each example.

Analyzing Persuasive Appeals

A persuader is trying to influence you. An effective persuader uses appeals that are designed to reach particular listeners. As an effective listener, you must be able to recognize and analyze these appeals. Then you can make up your mind about how to respond. In this section, we will examine the three major types of appeals that persuaders use. These are: (1) personal appeals, (2) logical appeals, and (3) emotional appeals. Although persuaders may combine these, we will look at each type separately.

Personal Appeals

An effective persuader first must persuade you that he or she is a *believable* person. A personal appeal from someone believable is often effective. Think for a moment about what makes a speaker believable to you. Usually you want the person to have a good background in the subject and to be honest and interesting. Of these three, the easiest to verify is usually a person's background or knowledge of the subject.

How do you determine if the speaker is knowledgeable about a subject? There are three ways you may gain a sense of the speaker's expertise in a topic area. First, you may know the person's previous background. Second, someone may introduce the person and indicate his or her background. Third, the speaker may refer to his or her background while trying to persuade you. For example, often you know something about people before hearing them talk on particular subjects. You may know that Ginny swam in the Olympic trials, so when she starts to talk about competitive swimming, you will find her believable. You may know Ed has been a disc jockey for many parties, so when he talks about popular music, you believe he knows the topic. You need not agree with these sources, but you know they are informed.

Introductions can provide background information. Suppose you had never met Chris before, but a friend introduces you and says, "Chris has worked as an ambulance attendant at Mercy Hospital for three summers." Probably you will listen carefully as Chris describes the need for more persons trained in CPR or cardiopulmonary resuscitation. Such an introduction provides believability for the speaker.

Finally, persuaders share their background as they are speaking. During a talk on sending foreign aid to Indonesia, a speaker may refer to his two years there in the Peace Corps. Another may refer to her work in advertising as she tries to persuade you to write and complain about a commercial. Others may tell you how they coped with illness, accidents, or drug abuse as they persuade you to avoid certain things. Usually the personal experience of overcoming a problem serves as a strong personal appeal.

In addition to knowledge of speaker's background, most listeners are interested in the speaker's fairness and enthusiasm. If a speaker appears unfair—only discussing one side of a very controversial issue, or calling the opponents negative names—you may get turned off. An effective listener wants to hear the whole picture, not just a very narrow view.

Unfortunately, even authorities on a topic can lose their believability if they use poor delivery for the messages. If a person appears timid and boring, or lacks enthusiasm, the listeners may get turned off or think the speaker does not really care. Effective listeners try to hang in there and get what information they can, but poor delivery can severely limit the listener's interest and attention.

Personal appeals may occur throughout a speech and may be linked to logical and emotional appeals. But if you do not find a speaker believable, you may not work very hard to listen for the logical and emotional appeals.

Logical Appeals

An effective persuader tries to organize facts and arguments in such a way as to persuade you to believe something or do something. Logical appeals refer to the ways speakers use evidence and reasoning to create persuasive messages. Alert listeners must be ready to question both the speaker's evidence and reasoning. For example, what questions might you raise about the following statements?

☐ ''The farmers of Nebraska will lose 70 percent of their corn crop and this will raise grocery store prices.''

☐ ''The Surgeon General reports that smoking can shorten your life by as much as ten years.''

☐ ''Fifty thousand people showed up for the rally demonstrating that it is time for a new style of government''. . .

☐ ''John's father assures us John is a fine worker and is a safe driver. We should hire him.''

Although each of these statements might be correct, you need more information before you could accept them as the ''final word.''

Evidence

Just as each listener needs critical listening skills, you also need an active evaluation of the evidence. By evidence, we mean the facts and opinions used to develop an argument. As a careful listener you can use the following set of questions as tests of evidence and apply these questions to persuasive information you are receiving. Then you can decide if the evidence is valid.

Tests of Evidence

1. Is the evidence clear, and does it have only one interpretation?

2. Is there enough evidence to prove the point?

3. Can it be proven to be true?

4. Is it consistent with itself (doesn't contradict itself)?

5. Is it consistent with other known evidence (isn't contradicted by other information)?

6. Is it relevant to the topic being discussed?

7. Is it the most recent information available?

8. Is the author/source of the evidence an authority on the topic?

9. Is the source unprejudiced in reporting?

10. Is the source trustworthy, honest, reliable?

Reasoning

In addition to examining separate pieces of evidence, the listener must examine the speaker's reasoning. Reasoning is the process of reaching a conclusion based on the evidence and the way the evidence is put together. Effective listeners should recognize the following types of reasoning: (1) reasoning by example, (2) reasoning by analogy, (3) reasoning from cause. You should also know the difference between inductive and deductive reasoning.

Reasoning by example is drawing a conclusion from several specific examples, instances, or cases. To be valid, this type of reasoning must meet three criteria. First, there must be enough examples: second, the examples must be typical; and third, the exceptions must not invalidate the conclusion. For example, a speaker may say, "SAT test scores have dropped in thirty-five states. They have stayed about the same in fifteen states. There is a national problem with student test scores." What is wrong with that reasoning? Another example: "The last four carpenters I hired did not know some very basic information. Training in this trade needs to be upgraded"

Reasoning by analogy involves comparing two things and assuming that if they are alike in some ways, they will be alike in other ways. To be valid, this type of reasoning must meet three criteria. First, there must be enough points of similarity; second, there must be more points of similarity than points of difference; and third, the points of difference should not be significant. For example, in a speech on seat belts, Lisa Sperling uses an analogy to describe the effect of using your arms as protection instead of a seat belt.

"There are much better ways to guard against injury resulting from a collision, people claim, than by strapping yourself and your friends into seat belts. One way that is gaining popularity with both men and women in this age of physical fitness is to build up your arm muscles so that just before impact you can throw up your arms onto the dash board and brace yourself with your arms in a locked, straight-out position.

For those of you who may be interested in this method of injury prevention, let me tell you the best way to practice. First of all, we'll have to try to simulate the impact of a car hitting something while going about 30 miles an hour. Not a very fast speed but we can build up to expressway speeds later. Go out and stand about 100 yards away from one of the sides of this building. Now run toward it as fast as you can. Go all out, building up to your maximum speed. When you reach the wall, don't slow down, keep running as fast as you can. Then throw your arms straight in front of you and stop yourself. You'll only have to try that once to see how effective it is."

Although many speakers use literal analogies such as the one in the speech on seat belts, others will use figurative analogies. Figurative analogy involves the comparison of two things that are basically unlike each other but have some similiarity that can be used to make a point. For example, one may compare the government to a stool in the following way. "Our government is like a three-legged stool. It has an executive branch, a judicial branch, and a legislative branch. If one leg breaks, the stool is useless. If one branch is weakened, the government will falter." If the analogy is not clear and obvious, a listener may be left confused and frustrated.

Reasoning from cause involves concluding that one event produces a second event such as a one cause results in a specific effect. There are four criteria for this type of reasoning to be valid. First, the cause must be relevant to the effect. Second, the cause must be capable of producing the effect. Third, there should be no other likely cause to produce the effect. Fourth, it must be likely that this effect is the only possible result of this cause. For example, "The burning lava rolled from the mouth of the volcano and destroyed fourteen homes at the mountain's base." In this example, the connection between the cause and effect is obvious and easy for almost anyone to understand. Yet if a speaker says, "The President's economic policies are the cause of inflation," the connection is not so easily seen. There may be other possible causes, and the effect of inflation may not be the only possible result of the economic policies. It is often difficult to create strong cause and effect arguments, but speakers try to do so. Listeners must use their thought-speed to consider other causes of the effect and to apply all four criteria to the argument.

Now let us turn to two other types of reasoning—inductive and deductive reasoning. Inductive reasoning involves drawing conclusions from specific facts or examples. A speaker uses the inductive organization pattern and describes a series of examples and instances and leads you to a specific conclusion based on this evidence.

The following is an example of inductive reasoning:

"Tom went to Puget Academy, and he received two college scholarships. Michelle went to Puget Academy, and five good colleges offered her scholarships. My niece who went there got three scholarship offers. If you want your children to get college scholarships, send them to Puget Academy."

In inductive reasoning the speaker moves from the specific instances to a general conclusion. But as a listener you have to be sure that those instances lead to the conclusion the speaker draws. If the speaker discussing college scholarships concluded, "Puget Academy has a great science department" or "Puget Academy is for weathy kids;" based on the three examples the reasoning would have been faulty.

Deductive reasoning involves moving from a general conclusion to making judgements about specific instances. The following is an example of deductive reasoning.

□ "As you know, all Democrats revere Franklin D. Roosevelt's policies."

□ "Tim Aragon is a Democrat, and you know what that means. If he is elected, we'll be back to the days of spending money like FDR did."

In this type of reasoning, if the general statement is incorrect, all the following points are faulty. Not all Democrats think that all of FDR's policies were wonderful, so we cannot conclude that Tim will follow those policies just because he's a Democrat. Yet some lazy listeners may not be alert to such faulty reasoning.

Read the following examples of reasoning and identify them as inductive or deductive. Then decide if the reasoning appears valid.

1. "Everyone I know from Hawaii can sail really well. I guess all Hawaiians are good sailers."

2. "Only Ozark flies from St. Louis to Raleigh-Durham airport. Martha was supposed to arrive from St. Louis. We'll meet her at the Ozark gate."

3. "The beach is filled with flies at this time of year. When John gets bitten, his bites get infected. I'd better bring bug spray."

4. "Rob met Candy at the Fourth of July picnic last summer. Cheryl met Ed there, also. That's a great place to find someone to date."

Listeners need their thought-speed time to play back the speaker's points and to decide if the arguments are valid. You must ask yourself, "Are these statements true? How do they actually relate to each other? Are the conclusions valid or invalid?"

Emotional Appeals

An effective persuader often tries to involve your heart as well as your head, by using emotional appeals. Emotional refers to attempts to tap a listener's feelings. Speakers may try to create a sense of anger, pride, fear, joy, or satisfaction in their listeners. These appeals can be very powerful because many listeners have strong feelings that can be easily aroused. Yet sometimes a speaker can overuse emotional appeals and leave listeners feeling manipulated or unconvinced.

Let's look at some general examples of how speakers use emotional appeals. A speaker on preventing child abuse may try to create a sense of anger or outrage in the listeners by describing a badly battered infant. A speaker on the dangers of high fat diets may try to scare listeners by describing the heart attacks often linked to such diets. Someone arguing to preserve the wilderness may appeal to your sense of joy as you hike through unspoiled forests. Finally, a speaker trying to convince you to send a child to Acme computer camp may appeal to your sense of pride in parenthood and your responsibility to provide your child with the "best."

A speaker who was trying to raise funds for a children's foundation described very vividly a mother watching her child dying of malnutrition. She said:

"I watched this young mother with no milk look at the limp body of her child. She stared at this child for hours on end with no expression on her face. Comprehending yet uncomprehending that in two or three more days the child would be dead. The baby remained listless and limp. You cannot watch that scene, even once, without saying, 'This cannot happen again'"

This particular speaker was most effective because she not only used emotional examples, but also used facts, statistics, and examples that supported her argument. She did not try to overwhelm the audience with sadness and guilt but rather she used personal, emotional, and logical appeals.

Read the following statements and identify the feeling(s) the speakers are trying to arouse in the listeners:

1. "Do you wish to see your child graduate from high school? Then put the cigarette down now."

2. "Thousands of your tax dollars are paying for your congressman's junket to the World's Fair. Do you really want to send your congressman on a roller coaster or a merry-go-round?"

3. "Picture the elk wandering through the forests undisturbed. Imagine eagles soaring overhead again. Can you remember a time when streams did not have animal carcasses in them? Raise the fines for poaching. Keep hunters off our lands."

4. "Club Romona is exciting. From the fast paced nightlife to the empty white-sand beaches, you are in paradise. Forget your troubles. Come play in our waves, walk our beaches, dance to our drums. You'll never be the same again."

5. "Have you ever donated blood? If you have, you know how good it feels to know that you shared your good health to help someone. What about rolling up your sleeves and helping to save a life? If you are eligible, come to the health office between 10:00 and 4:00 on Tuesday. You'll be glad you did."

When speakers use emotional appeals, they are trying to reach the listeners' feelings and bring you into personal contact with their subject. These are very powerful appeals, so you must use your head as well as your heart when you listen to a speaker who relies on emotional appeals.

As you know, most speakers use a combination of these appeals. Listen to the following selection from a speech and identify the appeals you find.

Smoke Detectors: Life Savers

A smoke detector is a valuable form of protection against fires. Most of the people who die in fires die, not because of the fire's flames, but from inhaling the poisonous gases that form the smoke, which precedes the flames. Smoke detectors give off a warning signal when there is smoke in a house.

As a fire marshall, I have entered houses and apartments to find brothers and sisters huddled together under furniture trying to escape the fumes and fire. Sometimes we have arrived on time to save these young lives. At other times I have caried twenty- or thirty-pound corpses out to grieving parents. These children were not given a chance. The alarm of an inexpensive smoke detector could have saved these lives.

You can purchase smoke detectors at most department stores. It is a good idea to buy a battery operated smoke detector. Batteries should be replaced at least once a year. A signal usually sounds when the batteries are weak. A smoke detector should be tested monthly, or if you have been absent from your home for a long period of time. This is done to make sure the detector is operating correctly.

More than 50,000 people will die and more than a million injuries will ocur because of home fires this decade. If you purchase a smoke detector for each floor in your home, you have a 90 percent chance, if a fire occurs, of getting away safely. Smoke detectors are inexpensive and reliable, if used properly. They are a safety precaution that you should have now.

In this section we have described the three major types of appeals a persuader might use to reach you. These are: (1) personal appeals, (2) logical appeals and (3) emotional appeals. Keep your eyes and ears peeled to recognize them.

Listening Lab

1. Have someone read the sentences in →*Listening Practice 41, page 116,* and identify the personal, logical, and emotional appeals used.

2. Have someone read the selections from →*Listening Practice 42, page 117,* and raise questions you would wish to ask the speaker. Or identify problems with the speaker's information or reasoning.

3. Have someone read the selections from speeches in →*Listening Practice 43, page 117,* and identify the appeals used by each speaker.

Recognizing Propaganda Devices

Finally we are down to the "nitty gritty." For some people the term *persuasion* conjures up images of the old medicine wagon with a phony doctor selling snake oil to the early settlers and using every trick in the book. Although much of persuasion involves appealing to peoples' needs, some persuaders do have a "bag of tricks" that they use on unsuspecting listeners. These "tricks" may be referred to as propaganda devices. They may be used for good and bad causes; they may make the speaker look foolish. That all depends on the skill of the listener. Although there are many propaganda devices, there are five main devices: testimonials, glittering generalities, name-calling, card-stacking, and the bandwagon.

Testimonials

Testimonials attempt to link a listener's positive feeling for a person, thing, idea, or event to another person, thing, idea, or event. We see the most common examples of this technique in advertising that features well known entertainment or sports figures. They endorse a product, program, or activity. For example, "Miss Piggy spends her spare time reading. Why don't you?" Or "Mean Mike Matlock eats Great Grain cereal before every football game." Famous people may talk for themselves. Bill Cosby may tell you the value of owning a home computer. Paul Newman may talk about supporting underprivileged children in Central America.

Every listener has encountered these and other types of testimonials. Your mechanic neighbor may tell you of the glories of his new sports car. A fashionable friend may tell you where to buy low-priced fashionable clothes. As a listener, you must be concerned connections and credibility. If there is no obvious connection between the person and the thing receiving the testimonial, you need to be careful. Miss Piggy doesn't really read and what is the connection between eating Great Grain and a football score? Yet since Paul Newman and his wife have supported a number of children in Central America, this makes him believable. If a friend recommends an exercise class but has not lost weight in six months, her credibility may be in question. If she lost fifteen pounds and looks and feels better, this may be a useful testimonial.

Glittering Generalities

When using a glittering generality, speakers provide sweeping general statements with which listeners cannot disagree. The generalization will sound very positive or very negative, but may not bear directly on the argument.

"Getting from one place to another in Los Angeles is torture."

"Vincent Peluzo is a wonderful family man. He deserves your vote Tuesday."

"America's schools are in a disastrous state."

After hearing each of these statements, what questions might you wish to ask the speakers? These generalizations draw a very negative or a very positive picture, but they do not provide a detailed or unbiased view. Let's look at each of them.

□ "Getting from one place to another in Los Angeles is torture." How many places did the speaker try to go? Using what type of transportation? What actually happened? How many adequate or positive experiences were there? How long was the person in Los Angeles?

□ "Vincent Peluzo is a wonderful family man. He deserves your vote Tuesday." What does being a wonderful family man have to do with his effectiveness in public office? What are his skills and educational background and previous political positions?

□ "America's schools are in a disastrous state." Which schools? All of them? Elementary, secondary, college? What good experiences are going on in schools? What gives this speaker the right to make that judgment?

Glittering generalities provide a sensational flavor to the overall message. Listeners tend to remember the generalizations, so you must be very careful to look at the evidence before leaving with any generalizations in your mind. As a listener, remember to ask, "How was that point supported?"

Name-Calling

Name-calling refers to labeling something or someone in a negative way. The speaker hopes that such language will cause listeners to reject or avoid the person or thing. The speaker's basic purpose is to create a negative impression. A clear example of name-calling can be found in this description of a city. See if you can identify words that create a negative image.

"The jobless squat everywhere. They erect bazaars everywhere. They plunk themselves even on 5th Avenue, to sell pathetic goods. They have doubled the ranks of the food vendors, hawking strange foods from increasingly unsanitary pushcarts."

Clearly thousands of words can be twisted into name-calling purposes. Some sample words that speakers use to label people or things in this way include:

weak willed	left wing	parasite
wishy-washy	right wing	naive

self-serving	Hitlerite	second hand
amateurish	subversive	well-meaning
misguided	wet behind the ears	over the hill
heavy-handed	overly zealous	worn out

Whether a word fits into the name-calling category depends in part on the audience. Whereas one type of listener would be pleased to hear a politician referred to as "right-wing," another listener would withhold a vote for such a person. As a listener, you need to use your critical listening skills to recognize emotional language. When you hear emotionally loaded words, you need to ask yourself, "What is going on here?"

Card-Stacking

Card-stacking refers to providing listeners with only one side of an argument. This comes from the expression "The cards are stacked in their favor." The speaker who presents this type of argument underestimates the listener's intelligence. Look at the following argument presented in a purpose sentence and see what you might wish to ask.

"This chemical factory will bring new jobs and a stronger economy to our town. It will therefore enhance family life in Waterville. Let me talk about each of these separately and I'm sure you'll agree with my analysis."

If this speaker only talked about jobs, economy, and family life in glowing terms, some effective listeners in the audience would start to ask questions about issues about pollution, increased traffic, and uncontrolled expansion of the town. If someone tried to persuade you to prepare for a career by only telling you the advantages, you should get suspicious. Only a naive person would try to persuade you to enter a hotel management career program by telling you about the travel, the choice locations, the interesting people you could meet, and the chances for advancement. A realistic person would tell you not only these benefits, but also the possible loneliness, the temporary poor locations you might work in, and the long hours. A wise persuader will list the negative arguments and will then refute them for you. That persuader does not want you saying to yourself "but what about. . .?" As a listener, you need to ask, "What is the other side?"

Bandwagon

The bandwagon approach suggests that you should do something because "everyone else is doing it." You may hear arguments with opening statements such as, "Everyone has one," or "We're all going to go," or "You don't want to be left out." Often you will hear commercials containing bandwagon appeals such as, "People in the know buy _____," or "Athletes who care about their feet buy _____ running shoes."

When you listen to conversations around you there may be comments such as, "Everyone is ditching school Thursday to go to the ballgame," or "The whole group will be at the concert Friday night." Sometimes it is hard to resist the appeal that promises you a place in the "in" crowd.

On the other hand, bandwagon appeals have been used to get people to take care of themselves. For example many health organizations have used the appeal with messages such as, "Smoking is out." or "Americans are eating less red meat and living longer."

As a listener ask yourself the following questions when you recognize a bandwagon appeal:

• Where do I personally stand on that topic?

• Am I getting pushed into something before I think about it?

Thoughtful listeners may decide to get on a bandwagon. Getting on a bandwagon should be your choice; don't let someone else push you on.

Listening Lab

1. Listen to someone read →*Listening Practice 44, page 118,* and identify the propaganda device contained in each one.

2. Listen to someone read the paragraphs in →*Listening Practice 45, page 118,* and identify the propaganda device contained in each one.

3. When you listen to commercials on radio or television, list in your journal the examples of the propaganda devices used by the advertisers.

As we said earlier in this chapter, effective listeners understand the process of persuasion, can sort out the persuader's techniques and make a decision about how to respond to the persuasive message. In this chapter we looked at the following areas: (1) understanding the persuasive process, (2) developing critical listening skills, (3) analyzing a persuader's appeals, and (4) recognizing propaganda devices. Keep alert as a listener. Don't be fooled by persuasive messages!

"If you love to listen, you will gain knowledge and if you incline your ear, you will become wise."
Sirach

CHAPTER 6 LISTENING TO FEELINGS

Introduction

Now we move on to what may be the most difficult type of listening—listening to feelings. In Chapter 1 we described listening as a "5E" process involving your ears, eyes, experience, examination, and effort. Now we can add one more "E" for empathy. This involves listening to another person by putting yourself in his or her shoes—by being sensitive to that person's thoughts and feelings. Because listening to feelings requires great sensitivity, it also requires great effort.

Feelings are emotional responses of a positive or negative nature that are tied to our physical state. For example, if you are angry you may experience increased muscle tension, a flushed face, more rapid heartbeat. As an observer you may notice those signs of feeling in a speaker, along with a change in speech pattern. If you are happy, you may experience high energy, a comfortable level of body tension, changes in facial muscles when you smile. Feelings involve emotions which are expressed physically.

To help evaluate your ability and willingness to listen to another's feelings, read the following statements and mark each one T for true and F for false.

1. _____ Sometimes I wish people would not tell me their feelings because I get uncomfortable and don't know what to say.

2. _____ I grew up learning that feelings, particularly negative ones, were private. I am not used to hearing people talk about their feelings.

3. _____ When people talk about their feelings, I sometimes make a joke or ask questions just to say something or keep the conversation going.

4. _____ I often find myself trying to solve a friend's problem rather than just listening to how my friend is feeling.

5. _____ I have trouble holding a conversation about sensitive topics such as death, serious illness, or problems.

6. _____ I often find that my friends come to me with their problems.

7. _____ I like to talk about feelings with other people because these conversations help me understand myself better.

8. _____ I find that my closest friends are people who share their feelings with me and I do the same with them.

9. _____ When I have listened to other people share their feelings, I usually feel good within myself.

10. _____ I find I get very tired when I try to listen carefully to feelings.

If you answered "true" to the first five statements, you have not had a lot of experience in listening to feelings. If you answered "true" to the last five, you are well on your way to being a person who listens effectively to feelings. In either case, you can always improve on your skill. To see how effective listeners respond to feelings, let's examine the following areas: (1) sharing feelings, (2) listening between the words, (3) listener response styles, and (4) reflective listening.

Sharing Feelings

As an empathic listener you are able to share the feelings of another because you recognize your own feelings and you can recognize messages containing feelings. The following is a partial list of feelings that you might experience or observe:

pleasure	discomfort	embarrassment
confusion	anxiety	fear
calmness	shock	numbness
disappointment	anger	jealousy
depression	happiness	nervousness
satisfaction	pride	loneliness
boredom	weariness	delight
fright	contentment	envy

Although we all have heard these feeling terms and have experienced most of these feelings ourselves, you do not often hear people say:

"I feel uncomfortable."

"I am happy."

"I feel frightened."

"I am anxious."

"I am jealous."

Instead, people frequently cloak their feelings in statements such as "I think. . ." or "I believe. . ." Instead of saying, "I am angry. . ." a person may say, "I think you made a big mistake." Or instead of saying, "I'm really happy to see you," a person may say, "It's really good to see you."

Sometimes people get so used to talking in such a detached way that they have trouble talking about their feelings. If someone says, "How do you feel about that?," a person may reply, "I think that. . ." But this person will not say, "I feel delighted" or "I feel afraid." In order to share another's feelings, you need to be able to recognize statements of feelings.

Unless you are able to get in touch with your own feelings, it's hard to deal with feelings in others. Sometimes we have to stop and ask ourselves, "How am I feeling?" It's one thing to say, "It's been a rotten day," or "I'm in a rotten mood." It's something else to identify exactly what is going on, such as: "Jennifer hurt my feelings when she was teasing me," or "I'm feeling lonely because my friends are away." You may even find yourself saying, "I'm feeling sad but I'm not sure why." Often the feelings you have experienced help you to figure out what is going on in someone else. You may use questions to help you figure out another person's feelings:

"How would I feel in that situation?"

"How did I feel when something like that happened to me?"

Although you may not feel exactly the same way as someone else in a certain situation, you probably have similar reactions. Understanding your own feelings will help you share another person's feelings.

Empathic listeners also have to recognize feelings statements. Look at the following list of paired sentences and identify the feeling statement.

"I'd rather not walk down the back road."

"Walking down the back road at night scares me."

"The end of the summer is not an easy time."

"Leaving you at the end of the summer always makes me sad."

"I told you not to wear my clothes without asking permission."

"I'm really angry that you borrowed my clothes without asking me."

"I am not looking forward to the auditions."

"I am nervous about the auditions."

As you probably noticed, the second sentence of each pair contained the feelings statement. That was the easy part. Most listeners can recognize a feeling when it is stated directly in a sentence. Your next job is to locate the feeling(s) hidden in more general language. This is called listening between the words.

Listening between the Words

You may have heard the expression "You have to read between the lines" which means picking up what is inferred but not actually said in a written text. The same thing can be done for dealing with spoken words. It's called "listening between the words," and it means hearing what is inferred but not actually said.

Many people do not say what they mean, particularly when they are talking about feelings—especially negative ones. As a listener, you hear a hint or a part of what is in the speaker's mind. But you don't get the whole story directly. The better you know someone, the easier it is to put his or her remarks into context. Recall the discussion about context in Chapter 2, indicating you need to know the person, setting, occasion, and the connection between the verbal and nonverbal messages. Look at how an understanding of context is necessary in the following situation. How might you interpret the following statement by a friend?

"I'm certainly not up for spending Thanksgiving at my father and stepmother's. I wish the day would just disappear."

Depending on your knowledge of the context for this person, you may interpret the underlying feelings as:

"I'm jealous of my father's time with his new wife."

"I feel guilty leaving my mother on Thanksgiving."

"I feel uncomfortable in their house. I just don't fit in."

"I feel sad not spending Thanksgiving with my mother."

"I feel upset watching Dad relate to this new woman."

"other:_____"

Only if you knew the speaker well would you be able to interpret the underlying feeling. You would know that the original statement about Thanksgiving was a surface statement. The strong feelings were below the surface.

Try to read between the lines as you read the following examples. Assign each of the following sentences to two different individuals whom you know and describe what feelings each person might be expressing. For example: "School is a joke."

□ My friend Tim would mean, "I feel bad in school because I never do really well no matter how hard I study."

□ My friend Eileen would mean, "I'm bored because I learned most of this stuff already."

What might two people you know mean by each of the following statements?

"I don't even think about the future."

"Lisa is a real loser."

"I wish my boss would get off my case."

"I'd like to go away and never come back."

Now try this with longer statements. When you listen between the words to these statements, you should find some feelings that were not expressed. Use the following questions as guides for uncovering the feelings beneath the statements.

1. What do I know about my friend that ties to the comment?

2. Is this comment consistent with my friend's usual statements?

3. What might my friend be thinking about?

4. How does my friend's background tie to the comments?

5. Does my friend have reason to feel strongly about this subject?

6. How might the occasion or setting affect what my friend is saying?

7. Do the nonverbal messages contradict the verbal ones?

8. What might I be feeling if I said something like that?

Now look at the sample statements:

□ "I'm in class with a real bunch of nerds and apple polishers. They hang on the teacher's every word and are always saying stuff like, 'Did you read about this in the newspaper?' I don't need this."

□ "My boss is always telling me, 'Watch Laura. She knows how to do it right. She's an efficient and courteous waitress. The customers really like her.' Well, if he knew what Laura says behind his back, his tune would change. I don't want to hear about Laura again—ever."

□ "Those people act like a bunch of kids; you'd think they were still in eighth grade the way they carry on. Think it's such a big deal to get together twice a year to party. You would think they could act like adults."

When listening between the words, use the advice of a wise person who says:

"Please listen carefully and try to hear what I'm not saying.
So when I'm going through routine
Do not be fooled by what I'm saying

Please listen carefully and try to hear
   what I'm not saying
Hear what I'd like to say
   but what I cannot say''

In this section we have examined how to recognize feelings statements and how to listen between the lines to recognize feelings.

Listening Lab

1. Note in your journal three situations in which you have had to listen to someone share feelings. Describe the situation and how you handled the situation. Then describe how you felt in the situation.

2. Someone should read the sentences in →*Listening Practice 46, page 119,* and the class should identify those that are feelings statements.

3. Have someone read the personal statements in →*Listening Practice 47, page 119,* and try to listen between the lines for underlying feeling in each.

4. Have someone read "I Was in Prison, You Visited Me" in →*Listening Practice 48, page 119.* Try to identify the numerous feelings that are found within this piece.

5. Create a statement containing disguised feelings and read it to the class. Ask class members to identify the feelings.

Listening Response Styles

If someone shares feelings with you, do you have a predictable response? Could you describe the ways in which you respond to feeling statements? As you know, the same feeling statement may receive very different responses from various listeners. Different responses can change the future direction of the conversation. To understand your typical response pattern, read the following statements as if a friend said them to you. In each case select the one response that is closest to the response you might give to such a statement.

"My boss said he has to cut my hours back to almost half time. That's not fair. When I took this job I assumed it was full-time for the summer. I am counting on that money for lots of expenses next year."

Responses:

1. "Why are the hours being dropped?"

2. "That's hard, but I'm sure you'll find a better job and you might even make more money."

3. "That certainly sounds unfair. People should keep their promises."

4. "You should go complain to his boss. Don't just give in."

5. "That's got to hurt. You take a job assuming it's full-time and suddenly it becomes part-time.'

"My Dad is really foolish. He's been smoking for twenty-five years, and every year he says he'll quit. But he never has the willpower. Oh, he's great at telling us that we can't smoke. He's real good at the 'do as I say, not as I do' routine. Someday it's all going to catch up with him."

Responses:

1. "Has he tried any of the programs for people who want to stop?"

2. "Well, maybe this will be his year. He's a pretty strong guy. He'll do it."

3. "I think you should keep on him about it. He really needs to quit."

4. "Why don't you and your brother tell him how strongly you feel about his smoking? Really sit down and level with him."

5. "It's scary to see someone you love take chances with his life."

"Everyone is always asking me about my future. What are you going to be? What are you going to study? Where will you live? What are your plans for this or that? And I feel I should have all these answers. Yes, Mrs. Trotter, I'm going to be a nuclear physicist who plays concert piano. No, Mr. Abramson, I'm not going to live in Greenville because I expect to live in fifteen different countries by the time I retire! I'm sick of it. Doesn't anyone want to know how I am right now?"

Responses:

1. "Why do you think they push you so hard about the future?"

2. "You'll show them. You'll be far more interesting than 98 percent of the people they know."

3. "That's a pain. People shouldn't push you about your life."

4. "Give them a joking response and change the subject. After a while they'll give up.

5. "It's really frustrating to have people constantly trying to push you about your future."

If you answered with the same response number each time, you tend to use a consistent response style when someone sends you a message with strong feelings. If you checked various response numbers, you may have different ways of dealing with these types of feeling messages. For the above examples, the response styles were all in similar order. There are five major types of response styles: (1) questioning, (2) supporting, (3) judging, (4) problem-solving, and (5) reflecting. Let's look at each one separately.

Questioning Response

All the number 1 responses involve asking a question. The questioning response indicates that the listener wants further information or believes that it is valuable to discuss a certain part of the point further. As a listener you may ask a question to: (1) get more information before making a different type of response, (2) keep from dealing directly with the strong feeling, or (3) get the speaker to think more carefully about something. Most questioning responses do not advise the speaker what he or she should do. Neither do they respond to the speaker's feelings in most cases.

Supporting Response

All the number 2 responses involve giving support to the speaker. The supporting response indicates the listener is trying to reassure the speaker. Usually the underlying message is "things will work out." As a listener you may give a supportive response to: (1) tell someone the problem will get better, (2) indicate that you care and that you have faith in the other person, or (3) say something nice because you do not know what else to say. Although the supporting response may reassure the speaker, usually this response does not deal with the speaker's feelings and does not provide solutions.

Judging Response

All the number 3 responses involve providing a judgement or evaluation about the situation. The judging response indicates the listener's approval or disapproval. As a listener you may give the evaluative response to: (1) help clarify the speakers' thinking, (2) reassure the speaker, or (3) indicate your values. Although the judging response indicates the listener's perception of what is good or bad, right or wrong, it usually does not encourage further exploration of the topic. It is found frequently in combination with the problem-solving response.

Problem-Solving Response

All the number 4 responses involve suggestions for dealing with the concern. The problem-solving response indicates the listener is trying to help or teach the speaker. As a listener you may use a problem-solving response to: (1) help someone cope with a problem, (2) make yourself appear useful or smart, or (3) avoid dealing directly with strong feelings. Although the suggested solution(s) may be helpful, usually this response does not touch on the speaker's feelings. In many cases, especially when the problem does not have an easy solution, the listener may make suggestions simply to feel helpful to the speaker, yet may ignore what the speaker really needs—a person to respond to the feelings.

Reflecting Response

All the number 5 responses involve an attempt to feed back to the speaker what the speaker is saying and feeling. The listener is trying to clarify the speaker's perceptions and feelings and to share some of those feelings. As a listener you may use a reflecting response to (1) help a speaker understand how he or she is feeling, (2) indicate your sensitivity to the issue, or (3) to check out if you are understanding the feelings and ideas correctly. The reflecting response to a feeling statement involves the listener directly at the feeling level. The listener does not try to solve the problem, explore the problem, or make judgments about the person or issue. The listener simply attempts to understand and share what the speaker is experiencing.

Each of these five response styles has value. Each encourages a slightly different reaction from a speaker. The effective listener chooses one response style, or a combination of them, based on the needs of the situation. If you wish to enourage the speaker, you may choose a supporting response. If you need more information, you will ask a question. If you wish to help the speaker, you may give a combination judging/problem-solving response. If you wish to be empathic and send the message ''I really hear you,'' you will send a reflecting response. Now read the following statements and imagine five possible responses covering the five response styles.

''I don't understand how someone can give an extra assignment a week before the final. I mean, we are supposed to take this final test in another week and he suddenly says, 'I want you to prepare a three-page analysis comparing the two main characters in the play.' What does he think we are? Does he think we have nothing to do but write papers?''

''My grandfather has been in the hospital for six weeks, and I'm not sure he will ever come home again. He has had cancer for two years and he seems to be really bad now. He had tried to be very strong for my aunt's wedding, but now that the wedding is over he seems to have given up. My grandmother goes to spend every day with him at the hospital, and I'm worried about her. She isn't eating and she cries a lot. When I was little, my grandfather used to take me for long drives and would play all kinds of games with me. Every summer I would spend four weeks at their house and we would go fishing. I can't believe he'll never get out of that hospital bed. I want to go see him, but I'm scared to see him. I don't know what to say.''

In this section we examined five types of response styles you could use when listening to someone express strong feelings. They are: (1) questioning, (2) supporting, (3) judging, (4) problem-solving, and (5) reflecting. Practice becoming skilled at using all five of them.

Listening Lab

In order to develop your skills at using the five response styles, try the following.

1. Listen to a number of conversations in real life or in the media in which one person expresses strong feelings and the other person responds. Note in your journal the types of response styles used most frequently. Tell how you might have responded to the same feeling statement if you were the listener.

2. In pairs, role-play situations in which you can experience the effect of different response styles. Ask person A to create a strong feeling statement and to share those feelings with person B. Have person B try one response style, and have person A react to that style. Then repeat with another type of response style. After you have experienced at least three types of response styles, talk about how each response influenced what A said next in the conversation.

3. Have someone read the feelings statements in → *Listening Practice 49, page 120,* and have class members practice using different response styles as they react to the statements.

4. Decide which one or two response styles are your weakest and try to practice using them in a conversation. Why is it hard to be honest about this?

Reflective Listening

When you tried to use the five types of responses described in the last section, you may have found it hard to create reflecting responses. Of the five response styles, reflective listening is used the least. And it is the most difficult response to create. Reflective listening involves giving feedback to a speaker on what you are hearing in terms of *feelings* and content. Reflective listening encourages the speaker to go deeper into the situation. It does not move the speaker on to new directions. When you listen reflectively, you are not taking charge of the conversation. Rather, you are letting the speaker determine the flow of the conversation.

In order to understand this, look at the following dialogues and see the differences among the situations. In situation 1 and situation 2, the listener actively determines the direction of the conversation. In situation 3, the listener uses reflective listening, and the speaker remains more in charge of the conversation.

Situation 1

Speaker: "This is a stupid assignment. Why should we have to do an analysis paper on the Civil War and have to use all those sources? It's due next Monday and I don't care. It's stupid."

Listener: "Well, look at it this way. You'll have to know that stuff for the exam anyway, so just do it and figure it will save you time later."

Speaker: "The exam is five weeks away, I'll never remember it anyway."

Listener: "Just keep good notes. What is your exact topic anyway?"

Speaker: "The Battle of Gettysburg."

Situation 2

Speaker: "This is a stupid assignment. Why should we have to do an analysis paper on the Civil War and have to use all those sources. It's due next Monday and I don't care. It's stupid."

Listener: "How many pages is it supposed to be?"

Speaker: "Between five and seven."

Listener: "Well, you always do well for Mrs. Jackson. She likes you. You can write something quick and just forget about it."

Speaker: "I don't think she even knows I'm there. I never say much."

Situation 3

Speaker: "This is a stupid assignment. Why should we have to do an analysis paper on the Civil War and have to use all those sources. It's due next Monday and I don't care. It's stupid."

Listener: "You're angry with the assignment and the time schedule."

Speaker: "You bet I am. I don't have 20 hours this weekend to do a paper."

Listener: "This is going to mess up your weekend."

Speaker: "It sure will. I don't read as fast as other people, and it will take me eight hours just to read the book. And then I've got to write the analysis. I hate it that it takes me so long."

As you can see, in the third situation the listener learned more about what was really going on within the speaker. In situation 1 the conversation moved on to the topic of the paper. In situation 2 the conversation moved to a discussion of the teacher. Situation 3 remained with the speaker's feelings.

As you try to use reflective listening you have to find the best ways of feeding back the speaker's feelings, or paraphrasing his or her ideas. Especially when you begin to develop this skill, it can sound awkward or phony. And you can overuse it. But it's important to know how to listen reflectively. Read the following short statements and try to create reflective responses you could use to pick up the speaker's feelings and concerns.

"The doctor is supposed to tell me this afternoon if the cast can come off this week and when I can play tennis again. After all these years I finally make the team and here I am sitting while everyone is out on the courts."

"My sister is going to Morocco for two years with the Peace Corps. It's really weird to realize I won't see her for two years. It's going to be strange around the house, since she and my Mom are so close and I've been close to my Dad. I don't know how Mom will deal with me after Andrea leaves. Two years is a long time."

"The cheerleader tryouts are this weekend and with my luck I'm going to fall flat on my face. I have practiced all the routines, but I don't have the same gymnastics background lots of the other people do. Maybe I won't go."

You probably found yourself trying to be supportive or trying to make suggestions for coping with concerns. It's hard not taking charge of a converstation. This skill requires that you develop empathy for the other person and try to put yourself in that other person's shoes. Not an easy job! But if you became effective at using the reflective listening style of response you will learn a great deal about the people who talk with you.

Listening Lab

In order to develop your reflective listening skill, try the following:

1. Have someone read the statements in → *Listening Practice 50, page 120,* and try to phrase possible responses using reflective listening.

2. In pairs, role-play situations in which you can experience the effect of different response styles. Ask person A to begin a conversation with a strong feeling statement. Have person B send a reflective listening response. Ask A to continue and B to send another reflective response. After two or three interactions, talk about how it worked. Discuss how well B was able to pick up A's feelings or concerns. Then reverse the situation and let B start the conversation on another topic.

3. Try to use reflective listening once or twice a day in your normal conversation and report on the effect of your comments in class. Describe (1) what was said, (2) how you responded, and (3) how the other person responded. Note how satisfied you were with the encounter.

In this chapter we have looked at these areas: (1) sharing feelings, (2) listening between the words, (3) listener response styles and (4) reflective listening. As you try to develop your skill at listening to feelings, remember the words: "Please listen carefully and try to hear what I'm not saying."

Conclusion

By now you know why this book is titled *Listening By Doing*. Listening is work and requires all parts of the 5E process—ears, eyes, experience, examination, and effort. Hopefully your experiences with the exercises in this book have paid off. You should be a more efficient and empathic listener. In order to consider your current knowledge of the listening process, retake the opening quiz from Chapter 1 and compare your current answers to your previous ones.

Read the following statements and respond to them as either true or false.

1. _____ You can't learn to listen. You are either good at it or you are not.

2. _____ Listening requires very little effort.

3. _____ The terms listening and hearing mean the same thing.

4. _____ Listening involves only your ears.

5. _____ Listening is an objective process. Your emotions do not affect your ability to listen.

6. _____ You tend to speak more than you listen.

7. _____ Good speakers are usually good listeners.

8. _____ You listen better as you get older.

9. _____ Your need to listen becomes less after you leave school.

10. _____ You listen primarily to get information.

This time your response should contain 10 F's. Now retake the listening inventory from the end of Chapter 1 as a way of analyzing your difference in skill level.

1. I am most satisfied with my listening skill in the following situation(s): _____.

2. I am least satisfied with my listening skill in the following situation(s): _____.

3. I have to work very hard when I listen to _____.

4. I enjoy relaxing and listening to _____.

5. I wish I were a better listener in the following situations(s) _____.

6. The type of speaker comments that turn me off immediately are _____.

7. The type of speaker comments that keep me interested are _____.

8. The nonverbal speaker characteristics which make a person easy for me to listen to are _____.

9. The nonverbal speaker characteristics which make a person hard for me to listen to are _____.

10. I listen to get basic information in the following situations(s): _____.

11. I listen to analyze the speaker's message in the following situation(s): _____.

12. I am willing to respond to a speaker with questions when _____.

13. I am not willing to respond to a speaker with questions when _____.

14. I believe I could be a better listener if I _____.

15. One personal goal I have in the area of listening is _____.

You should see changes in your answers if you have practiced the skills treated throughout the book.

Although no one is a perfect listener each of us can be far better listeners if we work at it. Don't take your listening ability for granted. Work to improve your listening ability and enjoy the benefits of your improved skills. The hard work of listening is worth it. Make a good listening a lifetime habit.

Listening Practice

THE LISTENING PROCESS

1. Introduction to Listening Skills

←*see p. 4*

The following are some simple ways to motivate people to think about their level of listening skill. The class should take out pieces of paper and prepare to answer questions. One person should read the following directions. The directions should be read once only.

"Number 1. If your name begins with letters between O and Z, make an X on your paper. If it begins with letters A to N, make a cross on your paper."

"Number 2. Draw a right triangle with the hypotenuse facing the upper right corner of your paper. Draw a star within the corner of the right angle."

"Number 3. If the numbers 2, 8, 16 and 32 added together equal 56, write the word rabbit on your paper. If they do not, write the word eagle.

"Number 4. Listen to the announcement and then answer the question. 'The Fourth of July Association will meet on Wednesday, June 18, in the Commons Room of City Hall to plan the parade order. Children's floats will be first in line so they do not have to wait. Floats with live music will be interspersed throughout the parade. Come help us plan the event.' Where and when is the meeting to be held?"

2. Using the "5 E's"

←*see p. 7*

Listen to the following statement read aloud, then use the "5 E's" *(ears, eyes, experience, examination,* and *effort)* to interpret the meaning.

"If you treat a person as he is, he will stay as he is; but if you treat him as if he were what he ought to be and could be, he will become what he ought to be and could be." —Goethe

3. Steps in Listening

←*see p. 7*

As the following statement is read aloud, think about its meaning. How would you respond to the speaker?

Learning Disabilities and Hyperactivity

Estimates of hyperactivity in children with learning disabilities range from 23 to 50 percent. In the general school age population, 3 to 20 percent exhibit hyperactive behavior.

Children described as hyperactive vary greatly both in the cluster of symptoms they present and in the related problems they encounter. The real question is "What is normal and what is abnormal behavior?" At one age or another most children are active, have short attention spans, display tantrums, lie, cheat, and/or exhibit other disruptive behavior.

Several studies of temperament suggest that high activity level, intense emotional reactivity, and distractibility emerge as patterns of behavior early in life and are relatively stable throughout childhood. Distractibility, aggression, and emotional immaturity seem to linger along with poor academic functioning. One researcher found 80 percent of the children initially diagnosed as hyperactive were academic underachievers five years later. Disorders of attention and concentration remained, but restlessness was expressed in less disturbing ways as they matured.

4. Social Rituals

←*see p. 10*

A. Role play an introduction in which one person, a poor listener, interrupts, misinterprets, and so on. Discuss the social rituals that the person is ignoring. A sample dialogue might start like this:

Charles: "Hi, I'm Charles Andrews. Are you here for the softball tryouts?"

Jim: "Hi, Chuck, I'm Jim. Yeah. I was on the team last year and I'm ready to go again. Last year we took second place in our division. I was rated as the most valuable player in six of the games."

Charles: "How many people usually make the team? Is there a...(interrupted)."

Jim: "They'll take almost anyone but only the good ones get to play. You know last year..."

B. Role play a conversation in which one person gives mainly one-word answers while showing poor eye contact and little facial expression. Discuss the reactions of the other person to this type of feedback.

C. Read the sample conversation of two strangers, mothers waiting for their children to finish a preschool gymnastics class. Use the following questions to start the discussion. Ask students to create their own version of this type of overlapping conversation.

Mother 1: "Did they go on the trampoline last week? We've missed almost two weeks because Molly has an ear infection..."

Mother 2: "Hasn't this winter been terrible? We've had sick kids every week. Jake had three separate ear infections and the last..."

Mother 1: "It's been a real mess. Molly's sister had dark circles under her eyes and a runny nose since October. I'm so sick of..."

Mother 2: "You just get one kid back in school and the other one is throwing up. It's never ending..."

Mother 1: "My doctor said there were two strains of flu going around and it was the worst winter in years for the week-long type of flu. Molly's sister was in bed for almost five days and you know that kids that..."

Mother 2: "My brother's little one was almost hospitalized. He had... Oh, here they come from the gym. Nice talking to you. Bye."

Mother 1: "Bye."

a. What appeared to be the purpose of the mother's conversation?

b. How satisfied do you believe the two mothers might be with their conversation?

c. How would you describe and rate their listening skills?

5. Listening to Understand

←see p. 11

A. Read the following announcements to the class and see how much people are able to remember.

Come to Beef Burgers Grand Opening!
1122 Hewlett Street, Rockford
Sunday, October 16

Celebrate with 15¢ hamburgers—Sat. & Sun. 2-4 P.M. only
Register to win a World Wide Vacations 4-day trip to the Rockies
Balloons for kids under 10—See Ricky the Clown
May 19, 12 noon & 2 P.M.

"The 7th Annual Southwestern Special Olympics will take place at Drake Stadium on Sunday, May 20. Volunteers are needed to help with publicity, decorations, refereeing, "hugging," and much more. Lots of ideas and manpower are needed for this special day—more than 500 mentally challenged will participate in this year's Olympics. A volunteers meeting will be held at 7 P.M., Thursday, April 26 in the Forum Room, Levere Hall, 2001 Sheridan Rd."

B. Read the following directions for employees in a fast food restaurant as if you were a boss instructing a new employee. Ask students to give you back the rules.

Guidelines for providing food in fast food restaurant

1. Get the drinks ready first—cold drinks, then hot drinks. Put a straw in the bag for each drink.

2. Place items in separately. Place down carefully.

3. Put napkins in for each main item. If main items are not ordered, put one napkin for each drink.

4. Place receipt in the bag and fold the bag over.

5. Hand bag to the customer.

6. Smile and say, "Thank you, please come back."

C. Read the proposed city ordinance newspaper article and ask students to answer the questions that follow it.

Ban on Video Games

The proposed city ordinance would ban video games in businesses within 500 feet of Middleburg High School. Video games are already prohibited within 500 feet of the elementary and middle schools in our city. The community residents who are members of the State Street Merchants Association favor the ban. John Marshall, superintendent of schools, said the young people were wasting time and money in video parlors. He requested the ban.

A lawyer, Maxine Kroll, spoke against the ordinance, stating, "High school students do not need these kinds of restrictions. They have the freedom to leave the building during lunch hour and they should have the right to use their time as they wish. The school has not been complaining of truancy."

The entire city council will discuss the matter at its next meeting on January 26. Members of the community are invited to share their opinions, but they must request a three-minute speaking time before the session. Community members wishing to speak should call the council secretary at 555-0067 before January 25.

a. What is the intent of the proposed ban?

b. What arguments have been advanced in its favor? Against it?

c. What should community members who wish to speak do?

6. Analyzing the Message

←see p. 12

A. Read the following persuasive message. After it is completed, answer the questions below.

Keep Life Flowing in Your Community's Veins

Has anyone in your family ever been in a car accident and needed blood? Do you know anyone who has had an illness and who was kept alive because other people cared enough to donate their blood? Next Friday and Saturday you will have the chance to help keep other people alive—and to help your own family in the process.

Next Friday and Saturday Midville Hospital will host the annual blood drive. Almost any healthy person between the ages of 17 and 65 can give blood. It will take less than an hour. It may be the best hour you ever spent.

Don't be concerned about the safety of the process. All needles are sterilized so there is no chance you will contract any infection. There is no danger to the donor. If you experience a slight dizziness, which most people do not, it will pass almost instantly. For the little pain and effort it takes, the high you experience from helping others will be a far greater reward.

If you donate blood this weekend, you or any member of your immediate family can receive up to five pints of blood over the next year. Consider getting this insurance policy for those you care about in your family.

Come to Midville Hospital, 2500 Grant St., between 8 A.M. and 6 P.M. this Friday and Saturday. Keep life flowing through the veins of this community.

a. Where and when is the blood drive going to occur?

b. What are the benefits to the donor for giving blood?

c. Why should the donor not be concerned or fearful?

d. How did the speaker attempt to persuade the listener?

B. Read the following sample persuasive message and discuss the following questions. Some students should create their own short messages with followup questions to read and discuss with the class.

Vote for Derrick

Vote for Derrick Henry as the treasurer of the Toastmaster's Club. Derrick has been a loyal member of Toastmasters' Public Speaking Organization for three years and he has actively recruited new members. Derrick has improved his own skills over the three years to the point where he won the local and regional speaking contests. Derrick Henry is one of the best things that has happened to this organization in years. His commitment and enthusiasm have helped to build our group. This year let's show him how much we appreciate him!

a. Why should someone vote for Derrick Henry?

b. What else would a careful listener want to know before electing Derrick to the office?

c. What didn't the speaker say? What do we know about Derrick's abilities or his record of handling responsibilities?

7. Listening for Feelings

←see p. 13

Read the following feeling statements and ask class members to (1) identify the speaker's feelings and (2) describe how they might respond as listeners.

"So what if I didn't make the varsity squad. Tryouts are just a big joke anyway. You either know the coach and are in the 'in' group or you're on j.v. for the rest of your life. Big deal. I know how good I really am. I don't need to deal with this place."

"It's going to be a rough summer. Most of my friends will be out of town and I've got to stay here to help with my folks' store. Tom is going to be in Mexico for eight weeks on a Spanish language program from college and that will be the longest period of time we've ever been separated. So it's going to be 'boredom city' for awhile."

"What do you do when your folks get into a fight? I mean do you just pretend you don't hear all those things they are saying or do you say anything to them? Do you ever feel you are older than your parents?"

"I've had a foster brother who has lived with us for two years and now he's going to be placed back with his mother. She's been in counseling and has some job now and thinks she can manage him again. I guess I should be happy for him—for them really—but it's going to be so quiet in our house. When we got him he was almost a year and a half old and he didn't talk or walk. He was undernourished and didn't smile or act like a kid his age. I taught him to say his first word. Now Ricky acts like any normal three-year-old. He giggles all the time and runs all over. He is even learning the alphabet. We've had foster kids before but they were older and they only stayed a few months. I don't know how I'm going to say goodbye to him."

8. Listening for Pleasure
← see p. 14

A. Read the following samples of amusing statements and ask students to give you similar examples that they have heard.

Excuses for Auto Accidents

"The guy was all over the road; I had to swerve a number of times before I hit him."

"I had been driving for 40 years when I fell asleep at the wheel and had the accident."

"An invisible car came out of nowhere, struck my vehicle, and vanished."

B. Have the students play a mystery story verbal game similar to those played by people sitting around a campfire. Have someone start a scary story and then stop midsentence. The next person must continue the sentence and build the story until all participants have spoken. Each speaker must listen carefully and build off the previous parts of the story.

Starters

"It was a cold rainy night when we first heard the clanking noises. They sounded like. . ."

"The house on Potter's hill has been haunted since the grisly murders of 1928. Many families have tried to live there, but each time. . ."

Listening Practice
GETTING THE MEANING

9. Meanings for terms
← See page 20

spelunking—exploring caves

shillelagh—Irish walking stick or cudgel

clogging—type of Appalachian step dancing

10. In the News
→ See page 20

Select one of the following news stories. Read aloud to one person; then have him or her relate the main points to another person.

Man Drowns Off Breakwater

The fishing had been so good all day Tuesday that Greg Patchett decided to try it again on Wednesday off the Vine Street Breakwater. After attending a family brunch, Patchett set out from his home for an afternoon on the breakwater. Long Lake police believe Patchett accidentally slipped and fell off the breakwater. A wind surfer reported seeing a body about 35 yards from shore off the city boat ramp at about 3:15 P.M. Wednesday.

The County Medical Examiner's office ruled Patchett died of asphyxiation by drowning. Patchett is survived by his parents, Lillian and Harold, and his wife Margaret. Patchett was a member of the volunteer fire department in Elyria. He worked as an accountant out of his home. Funeral services will be held Monday in The Village Church of Elyria.

Boy Snatched From Burning Car

A man snatched a young boy from the back seat of a smoke-filled car just seconds before the car burst into flames. The boy, Eric Tontello of 135 Main Street, is listed in fair condition in Janestown Hospital. He suffered smoke inhalation and burns to the arms and legs.

His father, Donald, had gone for help for an engine problem when he stalled on Greene Avenue two blocks from his home. Young Eric had just fallen asleep so the father did not wake him. A Greene Street resident, Thomas Fortas, was passing the car and noticed smoke from under the hood. As he looked more closely, he noticed a child sleeping in the back of the car. As Fortas started to open the door, flames started to shoot from the engine. Eric was strapped in his car seat so it took Fortas a few minutes to unhook him and pull him to safety. The child's father arrived back on the scene just as Eric was pulled free.

11. The Context: The Person

← see p. 21

A. Observe a friend closely for a two-week period to discover how his or her communication style changes under different circumstances. In your journal prepare guidelines for listening to this person. Talk in terms of how a potential listener should interpret (1) events your friend has recently experienced, (2) settings in which your friend communicates, and (3) certain occasions that have involved your friend.

B. Read the following comments aloud. Ask listeners to list possible past experiences that could affect how they listen.

1. "Our society has its priorities upside down! Can you believe an actor like Burt Reynolds earns the equivalent of $4,800.00 an hour while a social worker earns $8.00, a coal miner $13.00, a meat packer $7.00, and a pilot $33.00. These are estimates based on a 40-hour work week. Although we enjoy certain actors and major league ball players, there should not be such a great difference."

2. "Health care in this country is very expensive. When you just go to have a checkup, it can cost an arm and a leg. If you have to stay in the hospital overnight, it can set you back hundreds of dollars. In other countries a government subsidy makes it a lot easier to get treatment. Some people in this country do not see doctors when they should because of the fear of possible hospitalization."

12. Including Nonverbal Messages

← see p. 25

Read aloud to emphasize the nonverbal messages.

When You Lose Your Wallet

Oh no, It's gone. You just had your wallet and suddenly it's not there anymore. What to do? Each of us has gone through this scene but sometimes we get so disappointed or angry that we forget exactly what we should do. Here are some guidelines for dealing with the missing wallet situation.

1. Know your contents. Even before anything could happen to your wallet, know what you have in it. Photostat your credit cards and keep a copy of the numbers at home. Keep a list of what you carry around in that brown leather holder of much of your life. Be sure there is a current phone number in your wallet.

2. Look around. Very often you discover that you stuck it down in the folds of a purse of in your other jacket. Before you go through the trouble of dealing with a missing wallet, be sure it is really missing.

3. Notify authorities. Tell the store manager, the dean, the police—any authority that may be of help to you. Report the loss of a driver's license to the police.

4. Call the credit card companies. You must report lost or stolen cards, so you will not be responsible for purchases made on your card later. Read them the card numbers from the list you keep at home.

5. Get a new driver's license quickly. Call the secretary of state's office or motor vehicle center nearest you and report the lost license. They will tell you how to replace it.

6. Advertise your loss. Tell your friends. Put an ad in a local paper or school paper. Put notes up in message centers of a building where you lost it. Offer a reward if you wish. Someone may find the wallet and contents without the money. Someone may even find the whole thing. Be frustrated. Get over it. Get a new wallet.

13. Mixed Messages

← see p. 25

Read aloud each sentence at least twice, adding a mixed message the second time—through tone of voice or emphasis.

"This is my best friend, Robin."

"I'm looking forward to seeing you at the party Saturday."

"It's a shame you can't get the money for the ski trip."

"Have a good time, you two. I'll be fine here with my cat."

"I think it's great your boss wants to send you to California for a meeting."

"There's nothing else I'd rather be doing on a day like this than painting my mother's house."

14. Role Playing

← see p. 25

Role play the following nonverbal replacements for a verbal message:

Please sit down.	Come on in.
What time is it?	Hooray!
I'm starved.	I don't care.
What do you mean?	

Listening Practice

LISTENING FOR BASIC INFORMATION

15. Making Things Memorable
←*see p. 36*

Recall that the five parts of MTM are (1) change, (2) novelty, (3) repetition, (4) application, and (5) thought speed. Use one or more parts of MTM to present one of the following:

Parents and City League Softball

You may wonder why we insisted that any parents whose child wished to play on the City League team had to attend this meeting. Well, we're here to tell you just that. The City League philosophy maintains that sports are intended to develop skills and a sense of teamwork. Although there will be winners and losers in the softball games, this is not of primary importance to us. We are concerned that your sons and daughters get a valuable educational experience. To insure that this summer our young people will develop skills and a sense of teamwork, we will do a number of things:

1. Every child will play in every game and will play about an equal number of innings.

2. Children who exhibit poor sportsmanship more than once in a game will be benched until the next game.

3. Our umpires and coaches are other parents. They are not to take abuse from other parents. An abusive parent will penalize his or her child because the child will be benched for the rest of the game.

4. In order to prevent runaway scores, any team that is winning by more than three runs may earn no more than six runs in any inning.

This may fit your idea of athletics for children, or it may not. But it's how we play here and we wanted you to know the ground rules before the season starts.

16. Effects of Repetition
←*see p. 36*

Read these aloud and discuss the importance of repetition in each version.

Version 1

"I need you to babysit on Thursday, January 15, from 4 P.M. until about 11. Jeffrey will be in the soccer playoffs in the university stadium, so we have to leave early to get there and have dinner with the coach and other parents and team members. Tamar and Erin need to be fed and they need to do any homework. I'll leave dinner in the refrigerator. Tamar can pretty well take care of herself. You'll have to be sure Erin brushes her teeth, washes up, and gets to bed by 9. Also, she's on penicillin so you'll have to give it to her around 7 o'clock. If their homework is done, then they can watch TV until 8. I'll leave our phone number at the restaurant and the neighbors' number next to our telephone. Thanks. See you then."

(Now ask the listening group to answer the questions at the end of version 2.)

Version 2

"I need you to babysit on Thursday, January 15, from 4 P.M. until about 11. Jeffrey will be in the soccer playoffs in the university stadium, so we have to leave early to get there. That's why we need you by 4 P.M. We'll have dinner with the coach and other parents and team members. Tamar and Erin need to be fed and they need to do their homework. I'll leave dinner in the refrigerator. Tamar can pretty well take care of herself. You'll have to be sure Erin brushes her teeth, washes up, and gets to bed by nine. Try to be sure she does her homework right after eating. Also, she's on penicillin so you'll have to give it to her around 7 o'clock. If their homework is completed they can watch TV until 8:30. So, it's come at 4, dinner and homework, penicillin for Erin at 7, TV until 8:30 and bed by 9. I'll leave our phone number at the restaurant and the neighbors' numbers next to our telephone. Thanks, see you on Thursday the 15th."

(Now ask group 2 the following questions.)

1. Which child is to get the penicillin?

2. What time should you give it to her?

3. What date and time should you show up to babysit?

4. What is the TV schedule?

5. What are the two things you need to be sure that Tamar and Erin do?

17. Involving Your Own Interests
←*see p. 36*

Read this selection aloud and comment on how it relates to your interests.

Hug a Tree

If you have younger brothers and sisters, nieces or nephews, or children of your own, and they go hiking or camping, they need to know this. They need to know the "hug a tree" rules for safety. The National Association for Search and Rescue has five rules for kids who get lost while camping or hiking. Learn these rules and teach them to the kids you care about.

These rules could save their lives:

1. Hug a tree.
As soon as you realize you're lost, stop walking and "hug" a tree—that is, stay put. Searchers will look for you first at the spot where you were last seen. The closer you are to that place, the faster you will be found.

2. Take shelter.
It's easy to carry along a shelter that folds up and fits in your pocket. It's a big plastic leaf bag. Cut or tear a hole in the closed end for your face to fit through. Then slip on the bag like a poncho. Be sure to keep your face uncovered so you can breathe.

3. Save body energy.
If the weather starts to cool off, curl up like an animal in the cold. That will help conserve heat—your body's energy. Snuggle against a log, a rock, a hill, or anything that will shield you from the wind.

4. Make yourself "big."
Always carry a whistle when you go hiking. If you hear or see rescuers, make a BIG noise. Blow your whistle, shout, or pound rocks together. If you spot a search plane, stretch out on the ground face up and make slow, sweeping motions with your arms as if you were making a snow angel.

5. Remember that people are searching for you.
The longer you're lost, the more people will join the search. If you hear people yelling, don't be fright-

ened. They're exchanging information over wide areas, doing their best to find you. Remember, the searchers won't give up. THEY WILL FIND YOU.

National Association for Search and Rescue

18. Techniques for Remembering
←*see p. 41*

Listen carefully as someone reads the following sections. Describe specifically which memory techniques you would use with each.

Missing Children
The National Center for Missing and Exploited Children opened on June 13, 1984, in Washington, D.C. The center will assist families of missing, murdered, or molested children. It will also attempt to spread preventive information throughout the United States.

If a child is missing, the center will inform parents of their rights, be sure that the information is in the FBI computer clearinghouse, and provide advice on how to find a child.

Although children have been disappearing for years, this problem has been dramatized lately due to the national attention given to a few families whose stories have been dramatized on television. As the public became aware of the scope of the problem, pressure was brought to institute lifesaving moves.

For example, the Center will give very practical advice on how to develop and distribute posters with information about missing children. Such advice includes the following:

• Use photographs that reflect different poses. It is important to use more than one photo because people look different in different poses.

• Do not give only a police telephone number to call with information, because some people will not call law enforcement agencies. Give a citizen's group number, also.

• The poster should state that the parents are not interested in revenge or prosecution. Rather, they just want their child back safely.

The center will provide help to law enforcement officials, parents of missing children, and concerned citizens. It is hoped that this attempt to reduce the number of missing, molested, or murdered children will result in happier families across the nation.

Between Two Worlds
St. Mary's is an Eskimo village located on the Yukon

Kuskokwim Delta in western Alaska. The approximately 450 residents of the village are predominantly Yupik Eskimos, though the schools, stores, airport, and public projects have brought in a growing white minority.

The village stretches for about a mile along the bank of the Andreafsky River, four miles from the Yukon. On first impression St. Mary's appears quite Westernized. One can stand in the middle of either of the two modern "general stores" and imagine oneself in a White Hen Pantry in Illinois. Power lines carry electricity to most of the homes where children play Atari and watch movies on their family's video recorder. Snow machines, three-wheelers, and pick-ups pass by one on the road, past the newly acquired speed limit signs.

But in the same stores you will find the older men of the village sitting on the porch, chewing tobacco and speaking to one another in Yupik. On the snow machine might be an Eskimo man going to check his ice-nets or traps. As he crosses the frozen river, he might pass a neighbor's dog team. In the same house as the video recorder, there might be a grandmother sewing sealskin mukluks in the traditional way that has been passed on from generation to generation. It's likely that her grandchildren don't understand the language she grew up speaking.

The Eskimo village is a world on the meeting edge of two cultures. Change has come rapidly and dramatically to this part of Alaska in the last ten years, during the lifetimes of today's teenagers. They are of two worlds, wired into a Walkman, daydreaming of a seal hunt. These young people are truly growing up in two cultures.

Ann Diamond

19. Remembering under Different Conditions
←see p. 42

Listen to the following announcement read three times. See how much you retain as (a) a first-time listener, (b) someone who has heard of the sale vaguely, and (c) someone trying to remember prices.

"The store I work for is having a terrific sale on all clothes over Labor Day weekend. Most of the summer stock will be 50 percent off on Saturday, 60 percent off on Sunday and a full 75 percent off on Monday. Every hour they will have special announcement of specific reductions such as an extra five dollars off all sweaters for one hour. So you should all come to Brennan's on 43rd Street and Broadway that weekend. It's a cash and carry, no-return deal, but it's worth it."

20. Remembering Step-by-Step Procedures
←see p. 42

One student should read this slowly, and the others should attempt to recall it.

Heimlich Maneuver

1. When victim is standing, get behind him and place your arm around his waist.

2. Make a fist with one hand and place it, thumb side down, below the bottom of the ribs just above the navel.

3. Grasp your fist with your other hand and press in with a quick upward thrust.

4. Repeat several times if necessary, until the object is expelled from the victim's mouth.

21. Remembering Highlights
←see p. 42

One student should read this announcement, while others try to remember the highlights.

What the Journalism Program offers:

• Lab sessions will help students sharpen their journalistic skills and think precisely. Students will learn the mechanics of writing news and feature stories, editorials, and news for television and radio.

• Seminars conducted by university professors and distinguished journalists will range from "investigative reporting" to "the logic behind editorial writing."

• Workshops delve into newspaper layout, newspaper and broadcast news operations, writing for broadcast, and photography.

• Field trips take the group to Cleveland mass media, museums, and centers for the performing arts.

• Evaluation sessions provide one-on-one teaching by instructors who live with the students in the residential college dormitory. The student-teacher ratio is 10:1.

22. Remembering Details
←see p. 42

A. One student should read this very technical description of a football game. Have various students describe what they heard and the methods they used to listen. Discuss the effect of the technical language on listeners who could understand it easily and those who could not.

The Championship Game

What a game! The first quarter, Michigan's Porter kicked off through the end zone. Then Illinois gained two yards up the middle end. Stephans gained 10 yards around the right end. Then, as luck would have it, Riley intercepted a Gibbs bomb at the 32nd and Michigan had the ball again.

When Meyer had the ball, he passed for 13 and then for 10 yards to Aiken. There they were on the Illinois 45. Beck ran off tackle 19 yards to the 26-yard line. Then it was a mess. Meyer had two incomplete passes and a one-yard loss. Lee's 43-yard field goal was blocked, then recovered by Illinois at the four. But Scott fumbled it and Michigan's Harris recovered it on the 14. Covello gained eight yards outside, Beck swept left end for three yards, right end for three more. Finally, Meyer passed three yards to Aiken for a touchdown. Lee's extra point was good. So the score was Michigan 7, Illinois 0. And the rest of the game went along the same lines.

B. The teacher will read the following short news summaries and ask volunteers to remember details.

Four Win Lotto Millions

Four people beat odds of 3.5 million-to-1 and struck it rich Sunday by winning New York state's $22.1 million Lotto grand prize—one of the largest jackpots ever in North America.

State officials said each winner will get more than $5.5 million The winning numbers drawn Saturday night were 36, 22, 31, 3, 9, 38. The winning tickets were sold in the Bronx, and in Nassau, Ulster, and Monroe counties, said George Yamin, a state lottery spokesman.

The winnings will be paid out in 21 annual installments. The Internal Revenue Service gets 20 percent of the winnings.

Lotto ticket sales for the record jackpot topped $24.4 million, Yamin said.

23. Verbal Descriptions

← see p. 47

Someone in the class will try to describe what these diagrams look like. Other class members will attempt to draw the diagrams from the verbal description.

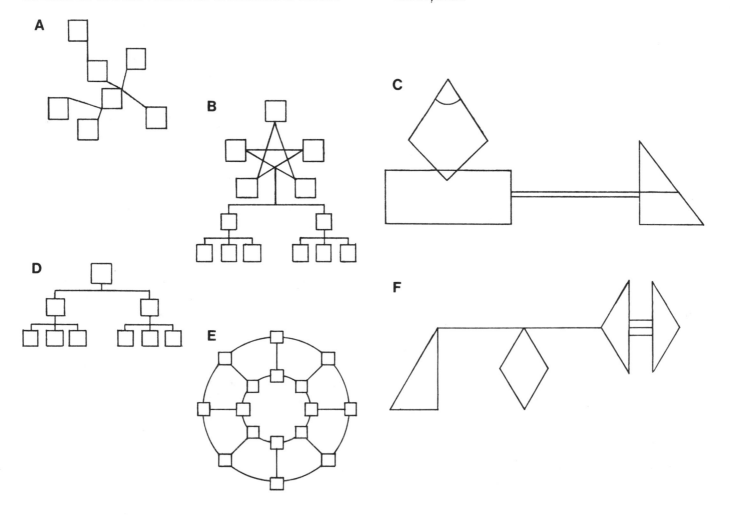

24. Listening to Rules
←see p. 47

After one student reads the rules, others should repeat them and ask questions.

Fast Food Station Standards

1. Check your appearance and wash hands before beginning work.

2. Speed up grill orders—have customers waiting for grills pull into assigned areas.

3. Single fold all bags containing food.

4. Be polite and smile.

5. Hustle at all times.

6. Team work is the key—back up others if possible.

7. Inform manager of problems with quality, service, or cleanliness.

8. Suggestively sell when appropriate, only one item.

9. Use clean towels only, and clean as you go.

10. Check stock frequently and fill as needed.

25. Listening for Details
←see p. 47

Students should take turns reading the customers' orders and remembering the details.

Restaurant Orders

Table 1
Customer 1: "I'll have the roast sirloin of beef, with a baked potato and carrots. I'd like a small salad with the house dressing and tea, please."

Customer 2: "I'll have the half a baked spring chicken, with french fried potatoes and cole slaw. I would like milk to drink."

Customer 3: "I'll have the chicken also but with mashed potatoes and the green beans. I would like just some tomato slices instead of the salad, since I can't eat lettuce. I'd like iced tea with sugar and lemon."

Table 2
Customer 1: "I'll have the large tuna salad, white meat, and leave off the egg slices. Plus I'll have a cola."

Customer 2: "I'll have the cold sliced turkey sandwich on whole wheat bread. You can skip the fries and just give me some applesauce instead. My son will have the hot dog with french fries and a choco-late milk. My daughter will have a grilled cheese with french fries and a hot chocolate."

Table 3
Customer 1: "I'll have the Artie Special—the three decker sandwich with turkey, pastrami, and corned beef. And I'd like an order of onion rings with that. And coffee with sugar and cream."

Customer 2: "That sounds good. I'll take that too but skip the pastrami and make it ham instead. I don't want onion rings. How about some french fries. And I'll have a diet soda."

Customer 3: "They eat too much. I'll just have a regular egg salad sandwich, no fries, and hot coffee."

Table 4
Customer 1: "We just want dessert. I'll have the blueberry cream pie. No, the regular blueberry pie with vanilla ice cream. And coffee."

Customer 2: "I'll have the strawberry cheese cake. Yummy. And coffee with cream."

Customer 3: "I've been dying for your Nesselrode pie—a big slice and hot tea with lemon and sugar."

26. Listening to Class Assignments
←see p. 48

After one student reads each assignment aloud, others should ask questions.

A. Social Studies

"Your name tells a great deal about you and may indicate things about your cultural heritage. What I would like you to do is to investigate the origin of your full name for Monday. Go to the back of the dictionary or to a baby name book and find out the meanings of your first and middle names. Ask your parents why you were given those names. Find out as much as possible about the history of your last name. Then include the name that you prefer to be called and explain why. After you develop a short essay, you may wish to create a small collage to go with the essay. I'll collect this Monday before class."

B. History

"Now that we are finishing studying the Civil War, I would like you to write an essay answering the question: 'What would our world be like today if the South had won the Civil War.' I would like to have you examine the social, economic, and political implications of such a situation. Rely on actual information from that period, and predict what might have been different if the outcome of the war had been different."

C. Mass Media

"I would like you to design a media campaign for a product of your choice. Design and produce an audiotape commercial for your product that conforms to the usual 30-second length and standards of taste. In addition, design a newspaper ad appropriate to the product. Design either a full-page or half-page ad. We will share these in class a week from today. If you have any questions stop by and see me. Remember, these have to be in good taste."

D. Grammar

"I want you to do all the questions on page 61 in the blue grammar book by tomorrow. We have talked about these areas and they should go quickly. If you have difficulty, refer back to the chart on page 52. I'll collect them before class. In addition, pick out four questions on page 62 and do those, also. That gives you a choice. We'll talk about those tommorrow. Class dismissed."

Listening Practice

LISTENING FOR STRUCTURE

27. Listening for Main Points

←see p. 52

The teacher claimed she made two main points in "Giving Feedback to a Public Speaker":
1. follow a formula of telling the speaker what worked well, what needed to be improved, and one or two things to do differently next time;
2. start with descriptive statements before you make interpretive or judgmental statements.

28. Types of Supporting Material

←see p. 54

1. (1)(5) The trees were toppled onto the road. Roots were ripped out of the ground. Thirteen foot waves rose on the lake. Andy and I went down to the breakwater to see the thunderheads roll out of the west. It was the worst storm in many years.

2. (8) Theologian Morton Kelsey once described listening as . . .being silent with another person in an active way. It is silently bearing with another person. I believe we do not give sufficient value to silence in our relationships. In a world of constant chatter, it is the rare friendship that can sustain quiet moments.

3. (9) There have been many breakthroughs in science which help us lead healthy lives. One is the discovery of the benefits of fiber in foods. If you base your diet on high fiber foods, you can lose weight and gain other health benefits. Foods high in fiber include

beans, bran cereals, cereal products, nuts, and dried fruit. Many vegetables are relatively high in fiber. So eat your corn, carrots, broccoli, and greens. Eat to keep yourself healthy.

4. (5) How often do you have your eyes checked? I certainly never thought much about it until recently. My last eye examination was eight years ago. I realized that when it got dark that I had trouble seeing the road clearly, but I thought everyone else did, also. I also realized that some people could read signs at a much greater distance than I could, but I thought they were farsighted. Recently, when I began to have trouble reading sheet music and seeing the ball during baseball games, I began to think that maybe I had a problem. I finally got around to having an eye examination and discovered that I was seriously nearsighted. I couldn't believe the world when I got my glasses—everything was so big and sharp and clear. So this was what other people were seeing all along! I learned my lesson. Regular eye examinations are an important part of caring for your health!

5. (8)(2) "How many of you have spent an hour in a car with a four-year-old lately? Raise your hand. Aha! And you survived! But you probably heard things like:

Kid: Knock, knock.

You: Who's there?

Kid: Apple.

You: Apple who?

Kid: Apple, banana, pear. . .Ha Ha!

After sixteen of these very strange "Knock-knock" jokes you are ready to scream. But next time think instead—"This child is practicing language skills." Maybe that thought will keep you from getting out and walking. What I'm really trying to say is, children need to practice language skills in order to develop their social ability. Therefore, parents, older brothers and sisters, and friends of the family must be subjected to all this practice. Just know that it will pass.

6. ___(3)___ According to a study cited in *Megatrends*, soon 75 percent of all jobs will involve working with computers. This means that all high school graduates must be proficient in using, not just familiar with, computers. In a survey of our senior and junior classes only 55 percent of the students had used computers and of this group only 28 percent believed they were proficient. This situation must change before today's freshmen graduate. This school district must provide a computer class for all students.

29. Purpose Statements
←*see p. 56*

Going on a TV Diet
Recently the A.C. Neilsen Company reported that American teenagers watch about three hours of television a day. Now this is less than the rest of the population watches but when you think about your sixteen to eighteen waking hours each day, do you really want to spend three of them in front of the tube? If you say "No" I have a suggestion for you. Go on a TV diet. It's actually a step-by-step plan to reduce the hours you spend fixed on the screen. Listen carefully as I explain the steps to you.

The Engineering Institute
Probability and Markov Chains. Digital Logic Design. Robotics. Do any of these words mean anything to you? Can you get excited about them? Do you have five free weeks this summer? If so you can attend the Engineering Institute at Alliance University designed especially for persons interested in careers in engineering. The Engineering Institute is a program taught by nationally known university professors who introduce future engineers to the many possible areas of study within the field. A summer at Alliance might change your life.

The American Shell
Americans are people in a shell. We grow up speaking only one language, but the rest of the world is filled with bilingual or trilingual people. When we travel, we expect others to speak to us in English. We do not make many attempts to learn the language or customs of the host country. Americans need education in foreign languages and in the customs of other cultures.

30. Identifying Supporting Material
←*see p. 56*

Risk It

Elissa McBride

Peter and Maggie Wanamaker had a home in Cleveland, two teenage boys, and a stable life-style. They also had a decision to make. Should Peter stay with his secure post in a Cleveland corporation, or should he accept the challenge of a partnership in a small insurance agency in Houston? Did being his own boss mean enough to him to take the risk of leaving his stable job and relocating his family?

After his wife, actress Patricia Neal, had had three massive strokes, an operation, and had spent twenty days in a coma, Roald Dahl had a choice. Should he accept the doctor's prediction that his wife would never recover from her vegetable-like state, or should he accept the challenge of helping her, mentally and physically, to recover? Should he risk the time and the effort of knowing that his work might never pay off?

A friend of mine, too, had a decision to make. Having always been an excellent student, she found herself, like most students in high school, eligible for four college-level courses her senior year. Should she accept the challenge of a difficult schedule when she might easily get A's in lower-level classes? Should she continue to push herself, or should she be satisfied with her previous accomplishments?

When faced with a decision like any I have mentioned, what would you do? Would you take a risk, or would you be content with the safe choice? According to a recent *Psychology Today* article, most Americans, when faced with a decision, "tend to pick the safer alternative." But is this the best decision, or should we be more willing to take risks?

First, let me define what I mean by a risk. When I say risk, I do not intend to invoke the image of someone climbing Mount Everest, or attempting to ride a motorcycle over a few trucks. Instead, I am talking about the challenge—the so-called healthy risk, and these risks are necessary in our society. A risk-free society would harm us in three ways: It would damage our economic system, it would lessen the value of our accomplishments, and it would minimize our ability to know ourselves. In the words of Thomas A. Murphy, Chairman of the General Motors Corporation, "Risk is not only an accident of life, it is an essential part of it."

Risk is essential in our economic system. Our capitalist economy is based on the assumption that prices will be kept down, by competition. Small, competitive business willing to take risks keep the larger ones on their toes. According to an article in *U.S. News and World Report,* "New industries and ideas are mostly created by people who are risk-takers." These risk-takers are men like Peter Wanamaker, who *did* decide to move to Houston and become his own employer. New businesses like his bring fresh ideas to the marketplace, and therefore force larger, established businesses to make similar innovations. As stated in *Time* magazine of Feb. 15, 1982, "New companies have become a vital source of American economic growth." This is the first reason why we must avoid a risk-free society.

Paul Recer, a bureau chief in Houston for *U.S. News & World Report,* related this story of two street beggars he once saw. The first was an old blind man playing a saxaphone. He shuffled down the street keeping up a continual stream of music. The only sign of his plea for alms was a small cup hanging from the end of his instrument, which was filled with the change of passers-by. The second was a carelessly dressed young man who had nothing but a voice that asked, "Could you spare a dime?" and an outstretched palm, which remained empty. According to Recer, "The old man was offering all that he had—a fading talent and a dying strength—in return for the silver. The young man offered only his need and the expectation that the need would be, and should be, met." The young man in this story was indirectly asking for a risk-free society—one without challenge, where one only needs to ask to receive something. You want to go to Harvard? Bammo—you're there. No preparation, no anticipation, no effort. Where is the value of an accomplishment if we don't have to put in any effort to achieve it? It is the striving that makes any goal worthwhile in the end. If you are challenging yourself to attain something, the achievement becomes doubly valuable. As Alexander Smith once put it, "Everything is sweetened by risk." This, then, is the second reason why we must take risks.

But what if our risk fails? What if, no matter how hard we try, we just can't attain our goal of, say, trying to stay awake in history all week? I know you're not going to believe this, but that's good too! Every time a challenge doesn't pay off, and we learn more about ourselves, the easier it will become to set realistic goals. According to social scientist Daniel Yankelovich, "Those who take risks rarely regret doing so, even when their choices work out badly. They feel they are learning valuable lessons." This is the final reason why we must avoid a risk-free society.

Okay—so now you're ready to take a challenge. But what should you challenge yourself to do? What is a 'healthy' risk? A healthy risk is one that is right for you. If you look at yourself and your accomplishments and decide that you can try to go one step further, then you are ready to take a risk. The risk itself could be anything.

When you decide to bake a cake from scratch rather than having Betty Crocker help you out, you're challenging yourself. After all, who knows how it might turn out! When you decide to talk a problem out with a friend rather than harboring a grudge, you're taking a risk. When you decide to try out for a part in a play, no matter how sure you are that you'll never get it, you're challenging yourself. When you convince yourself to try an honors-level course instead of a regular one, you are setting out to achieve a goal. If you or your parents decide to change profession or move to a new town, you are taking a risk. So risks can be as small or as large as we want them to be—as long as we do take them.

I've already told you that Peter Wanamaker decided to take the risk of moving to Houston. Roald Dahl also accepted his challenge. He set out to rehabilitate his wife—and succeeded. She is now more than 80% recovered. And my friend? She's still trying to make a decision—a decision like the one each of us must make every day: to be satisfied with our accomplishments, or to reach even higher and take just one more step.

Perhaps author Eda LeShan put it best when she said, "Although there are real hazards in saying 'yes' to life, they are inconsequential when compared to the regrets that come with saying 'no'."

31. Identifying Structure in Speeches
←*see p. 61*

Someone should read each speech aloud. Discuss the structure used for each one.

Speech 1. The Joys of Windsurfing

Every weekday evening and on weekends, Joshua and Sandy leave the office and head out windsurfing. No, they do not live in California. No, they are not terribly wealthy. They are people who enjoy one of the newest sports around—windsurfing. This sport has caught on throughout the nation, because it can be done in lakes as well as in oceans, it requires limited equipment, and it offers excitement.

Believe it or not, you can windsurf through the Great Lakes area and in small lakes throughout the Northeast and Southeast. More than 100,000 boards are sold each year and at least one-third of these are sold to people living in the middle of the United States. All you need is a little wind and some water.

Although the equipment is not cheap, it is a one-time investment. The basic board is around 1,000 dollars, and this includes the sail and the rigging. If you live in a cool climate, it would be worth it to invest in a wetsuit that will give you many more days on the water. This equipment is not difficult to store or to handle. No more hours of setting up the sailboat— just grab a board and go.

Windsurfing has all the thrills, gets you out in nature, and gives you a sense of motion and freedom. Whether you are balancing on the board or on skis, you are learning a sense of control and mastery. The mental challenge of either version is terrific.

Keep your eyes peeled as you look at your local lake or shore. You will probably see brightly colored small sails gliding along, with smiling people hanging on for fun and exercise.

Speech 2. When an Airplane Lands in Water

"We've got to ditch it." These are the words that no airline attendent ever wants to hear. And yet we have to be prepared for that very slight possibility. I have worked for an airline for six years, and no plane in our company has ditched during that time. But there's always a first time. So as a flight attendant, I have to be sure what the procedures are. I'll explain them to you so that if you are ever on a ditching plane you will not be as frightened.

You will hear about the possibility from the captain over the public address system. After the first warning you should do the following:

· Stop smoking or using matches. Put your coat on if it is near you.

· Take off your glasses, high heeled shoes, and remove sharp objects from your pockets.

· Loosen your collar and tie if you are wearing a suit.

· Put on the life vests as demonstrated. Adjust your straps so the vest fits snugly. Do not inflate the vest.

· Place seat in full upright position.

· Fasten seat belt tightly. Then go into the brace position. Usually you are directed to lean forward and hug your knees with your head touching them.

· As soon as you hear "Brace for impact," get ready for two shocks as the plane hits the water. You may also hear call bells to indicate you are about to hit the water.

· Stay where you are and don't even move until the plane has come to a complete stop on the water. Then listen to the directions for boarding the life rafts. Do not inflate your life jacket until you have left the plane.

This will probably never happen to you. But it is good information to know before you actually have to use it. Just listen to those flight attendants. They are prepared to help in any emergency.

32. Transitions

←see p. 62

Students were to identify the transitions.

"Let me review our air/regulations for you. All carry-on luggage must be stored under the seat. Hanging clothes may be placed on hangers at the front of the aircraft. Overhead racks are for light items such as coats and hats. We do this so heavy things will not fall on passengers during turbulence. As an additional safety factor, we ask that your seat belt remain fastened at all times unless you need to use the rest rooms. Your seat belt must be fastened during takeoff and landing and when the seat belt light is on. Also we ask that you do not operate a radio during flight as it might interfere with navigation equipment and it might disturb other passengers. In keeping with our concern for passenger enjoyment, we ask that you smoke only in the smoking sections. You may not smoke cigars or pipes. Smoking is prohibited during takeoff and landing. Finally, we ask that you remain in your seats until the plane has reached the gate and come to a complete stop. These regulations should make your flight safe and comfortable."

33. Transitions
←*see p. 64*
Read these selections for the transitions.

Local Photography Contest

There is a wonderful photography contest going on in your own home city. The title of the contest is "Friends," so you should submit a photograph that represents this theme. This is not a difficult contest to enter.

First you must be a resident of this city or a student enrolled in a school in the city. You must be over 18 years of age. You may not be a professional photographer. Then you must submit one, note *one*, entry—a slide or print no larger than 11 by 14 inches. This may be taken with any type of camera, but you must be able to provide the negative upon request.

Also, you should know that no composite photographs are allowed to be entered. Your photo must be a straight shot, so submit no variations such as double exposures. It's also important to remember to send your name, address, phone number, and a stamped self-addressed envelope for return. Mail the entry so that it arrives in City Hall by 5 P.M. on April 30.

Finally, if you or your family work for the city you are not eligible to enter.

The Future of Scouting

Most of us are concerned about the future of Scouting in America. There have been many changes in our society that have had an impact on a valuable program for our young people.

As a first example, we can look to the increase in the number of working women. No longer can Scouting draw on a large pool of mothers who led troops after school and were able to devote up to ten hours a day to concerns of the troop.

In addition, changing men's roles have changed the way fathers respond to Scouting. Many men now take responsibility for children and for the house in ways that are very new in our society. Such men may not have the same kinds of free time in the evenings for the demands of Scouting.

Another factor we can look at is the increase in the number of people living in the city. Although there have always been Scout troops in the city, there is a much greater need for urban activities and urban leaders.

Some of these changes can benefit Scouting. Sometimes three or four individuals or couples are taking responsibility for one troop. This means the Scouts may encounter many more unusual talents or hobbies. There is an excitement to rotating responsibilities for the troop. More parents know what goes on at Scouts than ever before.

Finally, the Scouts are adapting to the city. You see more field trips within the city, and you see cleanup efforts headed by Scouts. Scouts are getting involved in new kinds of social service.

So, although there are new challenges to meet as Scouting moves toward the 21st century, there are new services and resources available, also.

34. Prediction
←*see p. 64*
Read the following to one group of volunteers, with no predictive clues. Then ask the questions below. Read to a second group of volunteers, with predictive clues.

Sharks

Sharks have inhabited the seas in much the same form for more than 300 million years. Usually sharks consume a diet consisting of fishes, mollusks, and crustaceans. Few sharks actually hunt or eat marine mammals. Neither do sharks feed on humans. Most shark attacks are a "bite and release" attack or a slashing attack rather than an attempt to kill and eat a person.

There are more than 350 species of sharks. These creatures have a high sensitivity to electric fields. They are intelligent and can perform difficult learning tasks. They also have a good memory.

About one-third of sharks are egg layers. The rest are viviparous, which means they give birth to live young. Most viviparous sharks bear 6 to 12 young, but some varieties—like the hammerhead shark—produce 40 babies at a time.

In some Pacific Islands, parents allow their children to play in the water near sharks because they seem to have an awareness of sharks and shark behavior. They are able to sense when a situation could be dangerous and when it is not.

Most of us picture sharks as huge sea animals, but there are many small varieties. Sharks are fascinating creatures to study because they are so intelligent.

Ask the first group to listen for information related to the following:

1. whether sharks lay eggs or produce live young

2. the number of species of sharks we know about

3. why people like to study sharks

Now read it to the second group. Ask both groups the following questions:

1. How do sharks reproduce?

2. How many species of sharks do we know about?

3. Why do people like to study sharks?

35. Questions
←*see p. 64*

One student should read a selection; then others should ask questions.

America's Energy Concern

The United States is one of the richest nations on earth in terms of raw materials for creating energy. We have the world's largest single share of coal reserves. Even though we do import oil, we are the world's third largest producer of petroleum. Most people do not realize that we are almost totally self-sufficient in terms of natural gas. And we have the largest nuclear power output of any nation on earth. So where is the problem?

One area of concern is fossil fuel. The hydrocarbon fuels—coal, oil, and gas—which are trapped underground, are limited and we cannot replace them. The people of our century have used much of the fossil fuels built up slowly over hundreds of thousands of years.

New sources of energy such as solar and wind power are being developed, but this is a slow process. By the year 2000 our government hopes that 20 percent of energy will come from these sources.

Nuclear energy raises questions of radioactivity. Also, many people are concerned about the dangers of living near a nuclear power station.

People of our nation must be concerned with energy efficiency and conservation. This means car pooling, creating more efficient automobiles, heating buildings more effectively, creating better insulation. It means simple things like turning out lights and limiting the use of air conditioners. The issue of energy is a real problem and needs the attention of all peoples, in the United States and across the globe, in order for us to enter the twenty-first century with enough energy resources.

Listening Practice

ANALYZING PERSUASION

36. Coercive or Coactive Persuasion
←*see p. 70*

For each message, decide if the persuader is coercive or coactive.

1. "The Preparatory Nursery School provides your child with the foundation for a fine and prestigious education. Many college admissions officers tell us they look for our name on students' applications, because their attendance here tells the college a great deal about a child's family background. Parents who enroll their children at Preparatory Nursery School care about academics and care about their children's future. If you want your child to be admitted to one of our nation's most prestigious universities, don't set up roadblocks now. If you don't register your child at birth and enroll him or her at age three, your child will be behind in the race for the prestige university. Watch out for your child's future now!"

2. "Susan, the office group has decided you have a choice. You can stop smoking in this office, or you can look for another job. You must not endanger our lives with passive smoking any more. We are petitioning the management to remove smokers from this area of the floor. Sorry about this, but something has to change. Please stop smoking today or we'll have to say, 'It's been nice working with you.'"

3. "Susan, we have a problem. We really enjoy working with you and believe you should live your life as you see fit. Yet we are frightened about the effect of passive smoking on our lungs. Can we find some so-

lution that keeps up all working together as a pleasant group? We thought we could cover your desk for an extra ten minutes each morning and afternoon so you could go to the lower lounge and smoke there. How does that sound? Or do you have any other suggestions? We wish to continue to work well together, but we needed to tell you of our concern.

4. "We have come to the school Parent's Committee to request your help in sponsoring a blood drive among the parents of this school. As you know, two children in this school were badly injured in a car accident recently and they needed many units of blood. Luckily, the blood bank had the blood on hand, but now their reserves are running low. As each of us knows, any of our children could have an accident. The blood bank levels must be kept up. Although you may not know this, the blood bank's policy is to provide any needed blood free to the immediate family members of a blood donor on an annual basis. This appears to be a fair and generous move. Please help us get community members to take a few minutes to contribute."

37. Appeals to Needs
←see p. 70

For each statement, identify which human need is being targeted. Use Maslow's list of needs on p. 000.

1. "The aerobic classes will help you strengthen your heart muscle and may even help lower your blood pressure."

2. "At this college there is a great emphasis on support and spirit. People help each other and do not walk around as anonymous figures."

3. "At this college you will encounter great depth in each area of the science program. You will learn from the experts and you can work on independent studies under a professor's guidance. It's a good place to expand in your own directions."

4. "These refugee families need people who can speak English to shop with them and to go to the doctor's office with them. The children are very eager to speak English to Americans. Please give us one afternoon each week this summer to work with these families. You'll feel good about yourself and you'll learn something about being American in the process."

5. "Any woman needs to know karate to feel comfortable at all times. Although you probably will never use karate for self-defense, you will walk tall with the knowledge that you can defend yourself. Any potential mugger will sense this confidence. Classes start

at nine on Saturday."

6. "Come on. Everyone is going to be there and you'll have a good time. No one will care how well you swim or ski. It's a fun weekend and you'll meet some great people."

7. "The Great Books program is for people who wish to improve their minds and to understand their culture and heritage. It is not for credit and not for grades. It is for the person who wishes to grow mentally and who wishes to examine the world through exposure to the great thinkers. Sign up and widen your world."

8. "You won't need to worry about the next paycheck. Uncle Sam will give you a decent salary, training in a skill, education at no cost, and a good feeling about yourself. You can't do better than the military. Uncle Sam wants you—and if you have any common sense you'll want to join the armed forces."

38. Loaded Language
←see p. 75

Pick out specific loaded words or phrases in these selections:

1. "This is a bargain basement type of store. The antiquated dressing area, the outdated models, and cheap merchandise create a visit to the past. Only those with a nose for bargains should shop here."

2. "These are deserving students whose thrifty parents have scrimped and saved to provide their basic living expenses. The philanthropic alumni provide funds for tuition plus books."

3. "One day bulldozers with merciless jaws toppled the house and took bites out of the driveway. These tradition-eating monsters leveled a whole heritage in less than a day. The houses built as monuments to the dedicated zeal of immigrant railway workers fell before progress In the form of an expressway. An era ended in the rubble."

4. "The divorce rocked the foundations of our family life. The former spouses became tentative strangers. Weekends were a battleground as everyone sniped at one another. Some people moped, others attacked everyone in sight. Blessed time finally healed the rawest wounds."

39. Facts, Opinions, Inferences
←see p. 75

Someone will read the following sentences aloud. On a paper, mark for each sentence F for fact, O for opinion, or I for inference.

1. "It is a great day for fishing."

2. "The trout are snapping at the bait."

3. "We will have enough fish for supper for all of us."

4. "This is bad sunburn weather."

5. "I hate hot weather."

6. "It is 95 degrees and sunny."

7. "Mike said St. Louis was seventy miles from his house."

8. "We've been driving for an hour."

9. "St. Louis can't be far now."

10. "The library stays open until nine on Thursdays."

11. "Fred must be at the library."

12. "The union has 427 members at this plant."

13. "The union only had 310 members at this time last year."

14. "People are beginning to see the value of the union."

15. "This magazine costs three dollars."

16. "Half this magazine is advertising."

17. "Advertisers must sell a great deal through magazine layouts."

18. "The drought has lasted 21 days."

19. "We lost money in crops last year due to the floods."

20. "Dad will sell the farm soon."

40. Validity of Sources

← see p. 75

Indicate if the speaker is a valid source on each topic. If not, what questions would you ask the speaker?

1. "In recent years 20 suburbs have enacted laws holding parents responsible for teenage drinking parties. But the result is that many young people have moved their parties to public parks or to other places. The community should protect its parks."

Commander Malcolm Andrews,
Juvenile Division, Suburban
Police Department

2. "Lake Michigan has become the board sailing center of the Midwest. With 29 miles of lakefront and nine and a half miles of spectacular skyline, Chicago has over 2,000 sail board owners. It's the

place to come."

Adam Rosen, President, Chicago
Chamber of Commerce

3. "The Harvet-Powell desktop computer is designed with extensive memory and includes a large user-memory capacity. And it is a very portable nine pounds. It enables you to work with an enormous amount of business data. It's a good deal for the money."

salesperson at computer
company
or high school math teacher

4. "Hello, this is Jim Ferain. I'm calling long distance tonight. How are you? Have you considered a long distance phone service that will cut your bill in half? Can you imagine such a savings? At American Bell Incorporated, we have an offer you will never hear again. If you take the ABI offer we will cut your last year's phone bill in half or we will pay you fifty dollars."

ABI phone sales representative

41. Persuasive Appeals

← see p. 81

For each statement, identify the personal, logical, or emotional appeals used.

1. "When I was on a fact-finding mission in Thailand, I encountered members of the government who were concerned about the obligations of the rest of the world to the 'boat people' refugee camps."

2. "Three-hundred and eighty-five children cross daily at this corner without a traffic light. Only 200 cross at Maple Street where there is a light and a crossing guard."

3. "For those of you who do not know Benjamin Brown, he is our local Director of the Special Olympics. He is here to describe the needs for this year's Olympics."

4. "Picture thousands of baby white seals racing in circles as hunters leisurely bash their heads."

5. "Your money paid for these road repairs, which lasted less than six months. And the company says, 'This is a high traffic area.' This is nonsense."

6. "Over 1,000 Hmong refugees have settled in the Eau Claire, Wisconsin, area where schools have developed special programs to bring literacy to people from a pre-literate culture."

7. "When I worked on the first draft of this legislation, there was no mention of building a dam. Since then, special interest groups have gotten their claws into the bill."

8. "Would you like to send some poor children to the circus? You can add some real pleasure to their lives by purchasing five tickets at four dollars each and supporting the Summer Fun Fund."

9. "Dr. Ivan Kerlinger, orthopedic surgeon, reports that many joggers cause unnecessary harm to themselves by lack of preparation."

10. "I believe you would be more effective on your job if you took the managerial training course, which is offered on Tuesday evenings. I took it and learned a great deal. The techniques you learn should improve the ratings you receive from your staff."

42. Listening for Reasoning
←see p. 81

For each statement, analyze the speaker's reasoning. What questions would you like to ask the speakers?

1. "There is apathy in our community about school board elections. Last year 40 percent of the citizens did not know who was running. Only 30 percent of the voters actually bothered to vote."

2. "Don't go to the Outer Islands in March. The fog there is so heavy you feel as if you were walking in soup."

3. "Acme Driving School is the best place around. Ninety-eight percent of their graduates get a license. I had four friends who went there and got their licenses."

4. "The Barkers have a boat. They also have three cars. They are rich people."

5. "Since I gave up meat, my skin has cleared up. You should see if giving up meat would help your acne."

6. "The doctor said both boys' arms were snapped like twigs by the oncoming bus. Keep your hands in the window when we are driving."

7. "The Richards must have company. There is a camper parked in their driveway."

8. "It's not fair that our class should have to take senior year exams. No other class has taken spring exams in five years."

9. "Two people I know got skin cancer from being out in the sun and unprotected. We need to be careful about spending time in the sun."

10. "Three of Dirk Johnson's students have won state championships in track. He is the best coach in the state."

43. Persuasive Appeals
←see p. 81

For each selection, identify the personal, logical, or emotional appeals used.

There's a place for you at Olivetti Hospital and it's not in a sick bed. You can be just like Shelly Parks. Shelly is the outgoing, friendly volunteer who serves juice and coffee in the admission area and who can be found sitting with families in the operating area waiting room. She moved to this area 14 years ago to raise her family. Now that her last child is in school, she spends three days a week as a hospital volunteer. Shelly is a good listener who loves people, and that makes her job rewarding. "Every time I come to the hospital I'm happy," she says. "And I try to bring some happiness to the people I meet here." She gets great satisfaction from helping people. So could you. If you would like to share your life with people who need you, volunteer.

Dads, Devote Time to Your Kids
by The Rev. Clements
Principal, Holy Angels School

"What grade is your daughter in, sir?"

"Oh, I really don't know, Father. The wife handles all of that stuff."

"Perhaps you misunderstood me, sir. I know, of course, that your wife is ill and you are here to register your daughter in our school. However, we do need a little information. I simply am interested in knowing what grade your daughter is in."

"Father, this is what I've been trying to tell you. You see, the wife handles all of these things. I can't possibly remember all of that stuff. I got three other kids besides this one, you know. I can't keep all of this stuff straight. I better go call the wife at the hospital. She could tell you everything you want to know about the kids."

Suddenly it struck me that this man was only being honest and straightforward. He really did not know the grade his daughter attended, but more importantly, this father was not the least bit embarrassed about his lack of knowledge. He truly believed that this was "the wife's stuff"—no real concern of his.

I began probing. "Sir, before you make that phone call to your wife would you mind filling me in a little? Have you ever helped any of your children with their homework?"

"No, but the wife does all of that stuff. What's all of this leading up to, Father. I don't get the point."

"One last question. You already put down on the registration form that you work on construction. Do you think the guys you work with know much about what their kids are doing in school?"

"Father, to tell you the truth, I couldn't say. We never go into stuff like that on the job. Usually, I guess the wives take care of all that stuff."

I stopped tormenting the gentleman with these questions. However, the grim realization already had settled in that this man was quite typical of what is taking place in our society. An alarmingly high percentage of fathers feel precisely the same way he does. They firmly believe that education of their children is completely beyond their purview. As they put it, "The wife handles all of that stuff."

I, for one, vociferously challenge this myopic view of family lifestyle. The educational achievement (or lack thereof) of youngsters was never meant to be the exclusive domain of females. Husbands who relegate to their wives this extremely important facet of their children's lives are grossly irresponsible!

If family life is to survive, we truly must get back to the basic fundamentals. Fathers, Dads, Papas, let us redirect our priorities. You generated the child; now have the intestinal fortitude to shoulder your full share of the responsibility of raising that child. Your responsibility is on an equal level with that of your wife. To do less than this means that you are a poor excuse for a father.

Chicago Sun Times

44. Recognizing Propaganda Devices
← see p. 84

Read each statement below. Then identify the propaganda devices used—testimonial, glittering generality, name-calling, card stacking, and bandwagon.

1. "I know how you people feel. My Dad was a miner and I have always remained tied to my roots."

2. "Alcoholism is the American disease."

3. "A well meaning teacher kept defending the little delinquent until the state probation officer intervened and revealed him as a thief."

4. "Reggie Jackson subscribes to our theater season. Everyone enjoys the arts."

5. "Clearly the facts point to only one conclusion. I have demonstrated that this car is safer, more efficient, and less expensive than model X."

6. "An outstanding scholar, she led the competition throughout the chess tournament and captured the first-place award."

7. "Rugby is the sport of the future."

8. "When I am at the Capitol, I miss these mountains, the soil, and the people of this county. This is my home among the streams and pine trees. I know how people here think and what they need."

9. "I have found real value in cooking with gas," says Mary Phillips, home economist.

10. "There's only one side to this story. Child abusers have no rights and no reasons."

45. Propaganda Devices in Context
← see p. 84

Read each selection to see which propaganda devices are used and how effective they are in context.

1. "If citizens such as yourselves don't have the right to determine what is in our children's textbooks, we'll recreate a fascist-type state. Hitler got rid of the books that promoted traditional solid values and replaced them with narrow, prejudiced books. Textbooks are at the heart of our educational system. This curriculum committee wants to adopt a one-dimensional, non-traditional set of materials and confuse the minds of our children."

2. "We intend to speak about 'passive smoking'—the inhaling of smoke by nonsmokers. We think that no one has proven scientifically that cigarette smoke causes disease among nonsmokers. In a 1985 report, Dr. Robert Reynolds, an eminent surgeon, headed a special commission. The commission did not conclude that passive smoking caused cancer in nonsmokers. Passive smoking is not dangerous to our nation's health."

Arthur Scopes, Fillatron Tobacco Co.

3. "This community is becoming filled with latchkey children. Their parents do not care about their welfare, are devoted to the almighty dollar, and expect the community to provide the nurturing environment critical to a child's growth. When parents don't care, why should we? The latchkey syndrome is an epidemic. These children will eat our tax dollars, shoplift our stores, and drain our community resources. Douglas Duke, pitcher for the Temple Terrapins, remembers being a latchkey child and hating to return to an empty house. He says one parent must be home to greet a child after school. As one of the taxpayers concerned about our future and our limited resources, I say, send a message to the parents—stay home with your children."

Listening Practice

LISTENING TO FEELINGS

46. Listening between the Words

←*see p. 90*

One student should read each sentence aloud. The class should discuss whether each is a statement of fact or feelings.

1. "I am so pleased my Dad is coming to town this weekend."

2. "Tuesday's midterm test is going to be terrible."

3. "I feel that this kind of a job interview will be very pressured."

4. "This is excellent. We'll all meet downtown and spend all day Sunday together."

5. "I am so angry at Ted. He owes me twenty dollars and I can't get it back."

6. "We are going to the beach for the weekend. It should be beautiful at this time of year."

7. "Next week I have my final interview for the fashion training program. I'm really nervous about it."

8. "Are we really going to have to run three miles? I'll never make it."

9. "I'm really nervous about the biology midterm. There's too much information to get into my head."

10. "I feel that you should tell Mark exactly where you stand and not put up with the way he treats you."

47. Listening between the Words

←*see p. 90*

Read each selection aloud. Then discuss the underlying feelings.

1. "This is the first weekend in two years when I haven't had plans to be with Tom. We have been together for so long and it's so hard to realize I'm going to have to start dating again. It feels so weird. I mean, what does he mean when he says, 'I feel tied down?' I didn't hold his neck like a puppy dog. We each had friends. He's usually the one who gets upset if I have to go places without him. Now suddenly he needs more freedom. So he just decides this is the way it's going to be, and I can't do anything about it. I can hardly even look at him when we run into each other. I wish I never met him in the first place."

2. "You can call me 'Uncle Joe' today. I became an uncle this morning when my sister had a boy. And do you know what she and her husband named him? Joseph Andrew, after me. This is going to be one great kid. I guess I'm going to babysit a lot. But that's O.K. It's not everyone who has a kid named after him."

48. Listening for Feelings

←*see p. 90*

One or two students should read this aloud. The class should discuss the feelings expressed and those that need digging.

"I was in prison, you visited me"

I am in prison—for the rest of my life. I can never escape. No one can free me. I have committed no crime.

My prison is not made of bars and walls. It is one of flesh, bones, and blood. . .all mine. My body has become my prison. It never seemed like a prison when I was young. But something happened on the way to the forum! I became old. Why did I think it only applied to others?

The day finally comes when we look into a mirror with Snow White's familiar question. And the mirror answers honestly: we are no longer the fairest of them all. Is that really me? Why do I look so different from the way I feel?

Is there no solution to my dilemma? I told myself there were still things to do, places to go, and people to meet before I was ready to sleep. My flesh and blood prison sat in a chair, with a restless "me" inside, and life was passing me by.

How does one cope with sagging muscles, stiffened joints, aching parts which refuse to do our bidding even though the spirit is more than willing to go on? I never thought growing old would be like this.

The "me" who inhabits my prison has not changed that much. Inside, I wanted to take a brisk walk, go shopping, visit a friend, even do something daring, such as climb a mountain, swim an ocean, or soar to the moon.

Perhaps you are the answer. You can help me. Come to visit me. Let me smell your perfume. Bring the crisp, cold air of the outdoors inside to me. Play the music I want to hear. Read the news to me. Tell me about the world. Let's discuss a good book, a football game, the new look in fashion. I am hungry to know it all.

Above all, talk to me as an equal, rather than someone who has been reduced to basket weaving or finger painting. My IQ has not turned white, or even slightly gray. And please try not to look at me with pity in your eyes. My life has been gloriously full of adventures, joys, good times as well as bad.

When you must take your leave of me, refrain from patting my cheek like a small child. Give my hand a hearty shake instead. It may hurt my arthritic bones, but you will help me feel that I am still in the human race.

And come to see me next week. No appointment necessary.

Madeline Keen

49. Response Styles
←see p. 93

Someone should read aloud each of the following selections. For each one, the class should discuss how a listener might respond to the speaker using each of the five major response styles: questioning, supporting, judging, problem-solving, and reflecting.

1. "I'm so bummed. My dog got hit by a car when I was on a camping trip and my parents had him put to sleep. They didn't tell me when I called them, because they didn't want to spoil my holiday. I guess they were right, but Cricket's been my dog for ten years and I should have known. We really grew up together. I was still a kid when I got him and he was like a member of the family. I couldn't eat for two days after they told me. Everyone says I should get a new dog, but I can't picture ever finding another dog like Cricket. I don't know, maybe I'll change my mind after a while."

2. "I just got accepted as a senior counselor at Camp Dakota for the summer. I'm going to be on the waterfront and then live in a cabin with eight six-year-olds. I've wanted to be a senior counselor at that camp since I was a kid myself. I went there for five summers as a kid and then my family couldn't afford to send all of us to camp, so we did other things. But I always loved that place. I applied last year, but my application was too late. This year I sent it in two months early. They really knew I wanted to come. I'm

going to have to quit my job at the drugstore, and my Mom is upset because I may not get it back again— but I'm willing to take the chance. This is going to be the best summer of my life."

50. Reflective Listening
←see p. 95

Practice reflective responses to these selections.

1. "This is one of the best days of my life. Yesterday when it was time for supper my Mom called my four-year-old brother Sean to come in and get washed. But she couldn't find him. Then she called my sister and me to go look for him. We looked for about a half hour and we could not find him. By then my mother was scared and she called the police. They came over and started knocking on all the neighbors' doors. Soon everyone in the neighborhood was out looking for Sean. After two hours we were all crying and running all over. People worked in pairs and went up to a mile away trying to find him. Then more police came. Finally at about eleven o'clock my sister looked in the camper parked in our neighbor's driveway, and she found Sean asleep in the back. We all cried and hugged him. We didn't go to bed until two o'clock. I am just so relieved. We really thought something terrible happened to him."

2. "I think it's rotten to break off plans with someone just because you suddenly got a date. This is the third time this has happened to me and it really makes me mad. Pat and I had made plans last week to go to the movies and out for something to eat later. Suddenly I'm left with an empty Friday night because a better deal came along for Pat."

3. "I thought it was great that my mother was going back to work because we would have some more money and because she was really excited about it. She said it would mean things would be different around the house, but I never expected things to be so bad. Suddenly I'm in charge of dinner three nights a week, and I've got to take care of Sam from four until Mom comes home around six. She may be happier, but the rest of us aren't real pleased. I don't think it's fair that I should have to do so much."

4. "Mr. Norton just called and said I got a part in *The Music Man* this summer. I'm just going to be one of the townspeople, but at least it's my first role with that community theater. Anyway, I really like that show because it's so much fun. This is really great. How many tickets do you want? It's the first two weekends in August!"

Index

*Boldface type refers to pages in the Listening Practice sections.